BEHIND the *Mask*

A SURVIVOR'S STORY

Evangelist Vanessa Ford-Taylor

ISBN 979-8-89043-271-1 (paperback)
ISBN 979-8-89043-272-8 (digital)

Christian Faith Publishing
832 Park Avenue
Meadville, PA 16335
www.christianfaithpublishing.com

Printed in the United States of America

CONTENTS

The Deck Was Stacked Against Me

For I know the thoughts that I think toward
you, saith the LORD, thoughts of peace, and
not of evil, to give you an expected end.
—Jeremiah 29:11

I'm sure you have heard the saying "born with a silver spoon in your mouth" before, but this saying did not apply to me or my siblings. When I was born, the odds were not in my favor. However, the key word here is *was*. Now that I know my identity and to whom I belong, I walk in the favor of the Lord. I have come to understand that God's thoughts towards me are filled with goodness and kindness, and He expects me to bear fruit, fulfill my purpose, and achieve success.

In this chapter, I talk about the following:

- Mother having been imprisoned for murder while being pregnant with me (I was supposed to have been born in prison)
- Siblings having separated early and sent to live with Aunt and Uncle
- Humble beginnings not having much

- Mother having died when I was five years old
- Aunt and Uncle loving me but (however, I never felt it)
- Living in the projects (my aunt/mother would never let us go outside to play; she was very strict, and I always felt confined)

In the hot summer month of August, a woman gave birth to a beautiful baby girl named Vanessa. Alongside Vanessa, there were four other siblings, and later, another little baby girl. Things were hard back in the '50s and '60s for my mother as she tried to raise all these children with very little income. I often hear my older siblings talking about how difficult things were growing up. They didn't have nice clothes or always have enough food.

I didn't know much about my mother, only what I have heard. They said she was pretty and had a well-built body. She loved her male friends and enjoyed partying. When she became pregnant with me, she was already a few months along and had an argument with a man that upset her for some reason. Whatever the reason was, she was very angry. She was so furious that she went after the man. One of my brothers tells me the story of her coming home and telling them to stay in the house. Then she went into the kitchen and grabbed a butcher knife. He said she went outside, and he could hear her sharpening the knife. She then left the yard, and they said she went and fatally attacked the man she was angry with. She was subsequently sent to prison.

The three boys and my older sister went to live with my grandparents. Some months later, while my mother was in prison, she gave birth to me on August 7, 1964. I often wonder about her being pregnant with me, taking someone's life, and being in prison. I have always felt a strange connection to prison movies and had a desire to visit women's prisons. I suppose it was to somehow connect with what she experienced. I have heard people say that a child in the womb can sometimes feel the pain and emotions of the mother. I wonder what I was feeling as she took this man's life and what I was feeling as she was locked away from her family, carrying a child. I also wonder what my mother was feeling and what I had to endure. There is so much I think about that I guess I will never know.

After she gave birth to me, I was sent to live with my grandparents, who I heard spoiled me excessively. My sister tells me how she always resented me because when I came to our grandparents' house, I was treated differently. They say I had light skin with beautiful black curly hair, and everyone praised me. I was always dressed in lace socks and beautiful dresses, while she sometimes had to wear the same socks for months. I remember the day she told me about her feelings towards me. It felt as if someone had pierced me with pins. It truly hurt to hear that. I was just a baby who was born. I didn't ask to come into this world looking a certain way or even ask to be born at all.

The Master created me in the image He desired, so why did she have to feel that way toward me? I couldn't understand. Then I realized she was hurting. Every little girl wants to feel special regardless of our skin tone and wishes to be celebrated. Being the oldest and never experiencing that, and then having a sister born nearly twelve years after you, who receives the attention you've longed for, I could now see and feel her pain. We must be careful with our treatment of children, and the color of our skin shouldn't make a difference. In some families, it seems that the lighter you are, the more acceptance you receive. I find that notion absurd. Love does not see color, so treat me the same as you would if I had a different complexion than you.

I never knew my father, but I was told that he was an Indian. I remember one time when a tall, handsome, light-skinned man with curly black hair came to my grandmother's house. We were on the front porch, and he tried to give me twenty-five cents, but I was afraid. My grandmother told me, "Girl, you better take that money." I always thought that man could have been my daddy.

Eventually, my mother was released from prison, and she gave birth to my baby sister in 1967, three years after I was born. She passed away when I was just five years old, leaving six children behind. This is when the six siblings became truly separated. My three brothers went to live with my aunt in Pennsylvania, and my older sister lived with another family. My baby sister lived with my aunt, and I lived with my grandparents.

As I grew older, I can recall a time with my granddad. We were living in a trailer, and I loved Mountain Dew, which came in long-neck bottles back then. One night, during a severe thunderstorm that the South is known for, I cried for a Mountain Dew, but there was none in the trailer. Despite my grandma's protests, my granddad made up his mind to go out and get it for me. He went out in the pouring rain just to bring me my Mountain Dew. I stayed with my grandparents until the day came when, I suppose, it became too much for them to care for me. I remember being in the courtroom, where my aunt, grandmother, my younger sister, and I were present.

The judge had awarded me to be adopted by my aunt. I don't think my grandma understood, or perhaps she didn't want to lose me, but they both had me by the hand. Grandma was trying to take me with her, while my aunt was insisting that I should go with her. This is when I began living with my aunt. She had two daughters who also lived with her— my younger sister and her husband. My aunt's youngest daughter and I were only a year apart. I used to hear her call my aunt *momma* all the time, and I wanted to have someone to call mom. So one day, I asked my aunt if it was okay for me to call her mom, and she said yes. Since then, I have been calling her *momma*.

Momma and her husband were very strict. I never actually heard her say "I love you," although now that I'm older, I know she did. But in those days, you didn't hear that word so often. Her husband, on the other hand, was very mean and didn't care much for me. We didn't have much. We were on welfare back in those days, always shopping at thrift stores or relying on what people gave us. At school, I always felt like an outcast.

One morning, when I was in second grade, they came and got me from school and took me to the office. I was around seven years old and didn't understand what was happening. Some white ladies were talking among themselves. Next thing I knew, they had taken me to the bathroom, cleaned me up, dressed me in nice clothes, and combed my hair. I'm not sure what took place that day, but when I got home, I received the worst beating ever.

In those days, the welfare people would come and visit our house to check on how things were going. Maybe they had to do this because we were adopted.

The one time they came to the house, I was telling this lady everything. I told her how we weren't allowed to play outside with other kids, how we never got new clothes, and how my baby sister would get beatings all the time. I was just telling the truth, but when that lady left, I didn't want to say anything else because I received the worst beating ever. It was rough growing up. I used to hate when the weekend came or when school was out for the summer because we weren't like regular kids who could wake up and watch cartoons and play. We had to wake up and clean, clean, and clean. There were times when we had to walk all the way across town because her husband had some property where they were supposed to build a house or something. Every weekend, we had to wake up early and walk for miles carrying different types of tools so we could cut down bushes or weeds or whatever was needed. We would finally get there, but not much work would be done because they would start drinking and having a good time. Then we would have to pack up our things and walk all the way back home. It doesn't sound like a fun Saturday to me. It was the three of us—my sister, my cousin, and myself. We always played together. We had to stay inside our yard and weren't allowed out. We played hopscotch, jump rope, and we loved playing with old maid cards and jacks. Christmas at our house was different. We didn't have much even then. Momma always cooked a big meal with ham, greens, and all the goodies. We would wake up and find three little brown bags. Inside the bags, there would be an orange, an apple, a tangerine, nuts, and some candy. That was our bag for the day. We never got new things, only what was given to us for Christmas.

I do remember one year when someone adopted our family for Christmas. They picked our family from the welfare office and bought things from our list. That year, we received bicycles, the ones with the banana seats. We were such happy kids. I spoke about my aunt's husband and how I felt he didn't care much for me. There was a time when my grandmother was at our house, and back in the day, some people had to get their hair pressed with a hot comb. I never had to because I had naturally curly hair. On this day, my sister and cousin were getting their hair pressed, and my uncle came in, having been drinking, and started fussing, asking why they weren't pressing my hair. My aunt told him that I didn't need a hot comb in my hair. He got upset and said that I wasn't white, and I was no better than anyone else, so they should press my hair too. He would often fuss, and they would fight from time to time. Sometimes, if he said to do something, my aunt would do it, and this time she did too. I can recall her and my grandmother sitting there with tears falling down their faces because they had to put that hot comb in my hair. My hair was too good for a hot comb. He would come home many times drinking and fussing, which would often lead to arguments and fights. The next day, everything would seem okay. I used to always think that when I got older, I would take my little sister and get out of that house.

A Product of My Environment

- I started cutting out on school.
- I became out of control.
- I was hanging out with the wrong crowd, headed down the wrong road.
- At twelve years old, the streets was where I wanted to be.
- Mom called the cops on me; she became weary and tired.
- I was headed to a detention center, shackles on my hands and feet.
- I was let out of the detention center, and I was back on the streets.

Well, I am now around twelve years old. We have just moved to the projects. The projects were called Cross Creek Court, also known as Little Vietnam. To come up in there, sometimes you had to know how to fight. I began going to Terry Sanford High School. As I mentioned earlier, I was always like an outcast. I would get picked on because of my clothes or the way I looked, and I was so skinny. When it was time to go school shopping, we were at yard sales or the thrift store. Momma would get those clothes, bring them home, go through them, wash them up, starch them up real good, and then iron them up. On the first day of school, we were out the door to catch the bus.

When I was in the ninth grade, I met a group of girls who became my friends. These girls accepted me, and that was a good feeling. They wanted me to be their friend. That felt good. Remember, we were never allowed to play with other kids. One girl one day said, "Hey, you want to come over to my house?" Now, you know I did. So, I went home and asked Momma if I could go to this girl's house. She only lived down the street. My mom said *yes*. Wow, I was excited. Sometimes I think that Momma was getting a little tired. She had five kids of her own and then took my sister and myself. She had given birth to her last daughter when she was forty-three years old. But she allowed me to go, and this is when I began to be an out-of-control teen. I was like a bird let out of a cage. Freedom!

It was a Friday, and these girls were talking about going out, partying, and having fun. To a girl who wasn't even allowed out her front yard, well, that sounded like a ball of fun. I was like a bird let out of a cage! The place they were talking about going was Downtown Person Street. There were two little hole-in-the-wall clubs. One was called the Head Shop, and the other was called the Green Derby. That became our spot. There were about seven or eight of us. We were twelve- and thirteen-year-old girls in the grown-up world. You couldn't tell me anything. I had found friends who accepted me, and remember, I was that bird let out of the cage. It got to the point where my mom didn't say much, and I was going to their house all the time. Then when Friday came, it was time to hit the streets. We would go to one friend's house, and that's where we would get dressed.

Now, they had slightly better clothes than me, so they would let me borrow clothes.

There was one of my friends, and she was like a year younger, and I found out later that she was sickly. She was hanging with us, but we were about the same size and looked a little alike. She really had nice clothes, so I would wear a lot of her clothes. We would get dressed and do each other's hair and put on makeup. I remember afros were the thing back then, and even though I had very long hair, I would sometimes wear the curly afro and had to have the hoop earrings. We were too much and too young, hanging in the club with grown-ups. This is when I began smoking Newports, drinking beer, wine, and smoking weed. It became regular for us. I started to get a little smart mouth with my mom, and I started asking my momma for money.

I was getting older, and there were personal things I needed, and I wanted nicer clothes. She started giving us $25 a month. With this money, we had to buy our own soap, toothpaste, clothes, and everything. Now, even in the late '70s, early '80s, you know that wasn't much. This is when I started stealing at twelve years old. The girls that I hung with, we would go to the stores and take clothes and stick them up under our shirts and come out of the stores like we were pregnant, or we would go in with old shoes on, leave them, and come out with new ones on. This was our way of getting clothes.

I was still going to school at this time, but on the weekends, we would hit the streets. By now my friend's house was like my house. My aunt couldn't do anything with me. I met some guy who was in the army, and he liked me, but I didn't care about this man at all. We learned how to sweet-talk these men and get their money or a ride. Back then, I used to love Trans Am cars, and he knew this. Every weekend, he would rent a different color Trans Am to try to impress me. I was impressed alright. I enjoyed the rides in the car and would talk him into giving me some money so that I could buy myself things. I never slept with the man, just used him to get what I needed. Us girls continued to hang out on the weekend. We would go down there and party. I remember the dance called "Baby Doll" was out. I thought I was getting down doing that dance. The song "Firecracker" and Michael Jackson's song "Don't Stop 'Til You Get Enough" were my songs. I would hear them come on the jukebox and would dance forever. The movie *Sparkle* was out back then, and I remember that we would pool our dollars together and our crew would go to see it. Oh, that was an all-time favorite. We all thought that we were someone in the movies. I always thought I was Sister, and later on in my life, it seemed as if I was her. Oh, but how much fun it would be. We would be walking home singing and acting as if we were in the movie. Now, some of the things that I didn't have before, I now felt I had. Remember, I never had friends, never felt accepted, and the biggest thing of all is I just wanted to feel love and, most of all, to hear those words.

My First Love

I met my first love when I was thirteen, and he was twenty-three. He was very good-looking, tall, dark, and handsome. Our hangout spot was the juke joint downtown, and I got into fights with other girls over him. He told me he loved me, and that's all I wanted to hear. However, one day he came to the house drunk and got into a fight, breaking a glass over his head. Later on, he went to prison.

Now I'm thirteen and still hanging out on Person Street. One night, there was a tall, brown-skinned man wearing a hat that I called the "apple hat." Wow, he was fine. He had a beautiful smile, and when he stood up, he was so bowlegged and sexy. This man kept smiling at me, and to tell the truth, I think I fell in love with him then. He became my first love. I was thirteen, and he was twenty-three. I didn't know anything about sex, but now I had a man who was ten years older than me introducing me to it. He slowly moved on to me and stole my heart, and he said the words I was looking for: *I love you*. That night came when, as Betty Wright sings, "Tonight is the night that you make me a woman." We were at the club, drinking, and the moment came when we left and drove down a dark road, and that night I lost my virginity.

Now I think back and ask myself, Why would a twenty-three-year-old man want to be with a thirteen-year-old girl? I think he saw a girl who was vulnerable and took advantage of her. I just wanted to be loved. Sadly, we still see this happen so many times in life today. Young girls are looking for love and for someone to take care of them, and they come across these guys who are out there looking for this type of girl to take advantage of. Some girls don't even make it out of situations like this in their right mind or even alive. It's so important that we teach our girls that love isn't found in the streets or in having sex with a man. I now believe that love starts with ourselves. We have to learn to love ourselves first. If we were to do this, we may not find ourselves in some of the relationships that we do. We would think higher of ourselves and tell ourselves that we are better than that. I didn't know this back then. I didn't have anyone to tell me these things, to tell me that I am as precious as a diamond and that I don't need to give myself up like that, but to wait for the right person and the right time, and that person will treat me and my needs like a jeweler cares for a diamond.

After that night, he had blown my mind. I was in love with this man. He was my world. I couldn't wait to see him. You know how we are when we meet the man we fall in love with—you cannot stand to be a moment apart. He was like honey, and I was the bee. I remember our song by G.Q., "I Do Love You." I'm in the ninth grade now, but my grades are bad. I have started drinking, smoking weed, and cigarettes. I would catch the bus to school, eat breakfast, and sneak out of school. We would leave and walk downtown to the headshop to see my man and get high. Then we would walk back to school in time to catch the bus back home. It was the end of the school year, and I failed the ninth grade. Well, I didn't care because by now it was all about hanging out and my love. When school resumed, I went back, but I was so out of control that I ended up getting kicked out of school. I left there with over two hundred detention hours. Even my brother came all the way from Pennsylvania to try to put me back in school, but the day he left, I skipped school and was hanging back downtown. I went to another school and was there for like three days, but they kicked me out as well. I guess they were a little intimidated by my appearance for a ninth grader. So I just dropped out of school in the ninth grade and left home. I stayed wherever my boyfriend and I ended up that night or with one of my friends.

One day, my aunt tricked me. It was a Friday, and my cousin sent word that my aunt was very sick or something, and I needed to come home. Well, I had just gotten my hair all done up and went to the house, and there were the police waiting for me. My mom had called the cops on me because I had left home, and they hadn't seen me. I was so skinny back then that the handcuffs would fall off my hands, so they had to handcuff my hands in the front, and they put me in the front of the police car and took me to a detention center. I had to stay there for like thirty days. It was up to my aunt to decide if I should come home. She asked me if I promised that I would get back in school and stay out of those streets. If I made that promise, she would allow me to come home.

Well, the morning came for me and the other kids to go before the judge. I remember we were all cuffed together and brought into the courtroom. The judge asked me if I would keep these promises to my mom. Of course, I said yes, and I was free to go. I went home with my mom, and then I heard from someone that my man was sleeping around with some girl. My mom needed something from the store, so I told her I would go get it. I took that money and went straight downtown. She didn't see me for a while. That night, I went to fight. This is also when domestic violence began in my life. I found out that the man I was so in love with had two other older women, and both had kids. He was a player. Some Friday nights, I had to be ready to fight because one of the ladies would come down to the club and want to know where he had been. We would start going at each other, and sometimes the cops were called to break it up, or I would get kicked out of the bar for a few days. The owner of the bar was so fond of us girls that he would let me back in, but I felt that although he may have had two other women, I was now the main one. He was with me all the time.

This is also when domestic violence started in our life. I heard that he would beat up the other girl, but I thought he wouldn't do that to me. However, he had beaten her up so badly and thrown her out of a window. She went to stay with her mother for a few days so that she could have help taking care of their son. He took me one night to stay at her house. I loved him so much that I went to stay. We had lots of fights too. I remember one time he slapped me so hard that I blacked out, and when I woke up, I was on the other side of the street. It began with black eyes and bruises. I was fourteen years old and getting beaten up by a twenty-four-year-old man. Not only was I getting beat up, but he also cheated on me. But whenever he said, "I love you, and I'm sorry," I would go back to him. I went back home to stay some nights, and there was this one night I remember when he came to the house and he was on something. His eyes looked glazed, and he wanted me to come with him, but I didn't want to. He started trying to pull me out the door, and then he came into the house, and we began to fight.

The fight ended in my bedroom, and I picked up a mirror that wasn't attached to the dresser and broke it across his head, cutting him across the forehead. He was arrested and taken to jail, and the next day I was down there trying to bail him out because I loved him, blinded by love. I stayed with him until the age of sixteen, still getting beat up, drinking, and getting high, still thinking I'm in love. I guess what we want sometimes is not what God wants for us. I really wanted to have a child by him. These other women had a child, and that's what I wanted, but God had a different plan. Thank you, LORD!

From One Relationship to the Next

I met a new man, also older, and we started a relationship. It quickly became a whirlwind relationship characterized by verbal and physical abuse. I became pregnant early on and had two kids by the hands of my abuser. This man had a Dr. Jekyll and Mr. Hyde personality.

At sixteen years old, my first love and I had been together for three and a half years. He got into trouble and had to spend some time in prison, which devastated me. I remember being so upset on Thanksgiving that I got drunk and tried to kill myself by taking an overdose of pills. It's ridiculous how we can do such foolish things over a man, but that's what I did. I woke up in a mental health facility and had to stay there for a few weeks until they deemed me okay. Interestingly enough, I made some friends in there, and we had a great time. One of the girls would leave to go to work or something and she would bring back some weed for us to get high. We would also tease a guy in there, taking some tobacco out of his cigarettes, putting in matches, and watching him light the cigarette only for it to blow up and him to jump up screaming. I'm really surprised I made it out of that place. Once I was released, I started hanging out downtown again.

During this time, I was briefly involved with a man who was older and had a good job. He was married and had two little boys, but he and his wife were separated. He took good care of me. My mom was quite fond of him, and whenever he visited, she expected him to bring her a box of snuff and a six-pack of beer. He also bought us hot food to eat when we didn't have electricity at home or couldn't cook because of our electric stove. Although our time together was short, he was kind to me. I remember a favorite song of his was "Lady" by the Whispers. Eventually, he moved away, and that's when I met the man who became the father of my two older children. I had seen him around before as we all hung out at the same place. He, too, was ten years older than me.

As I mentioned, I had seen him before and always thought he looked neat. He was handsome, tall, and had dark skin. He was always well-groomed, with a nice haircut. We started noticing each other, and one day we began talking. Word got out to my first love that I was seeing him, and he sent a message that he would get his Vanessa back when he got out. Nevertheless, I started dating this new man. Things were great. He was a hard worker and seemed well put together. I often tell women that these men don't come with signs saying, "Hey, I am a woman beater." You would think that after experiencing the abuse I just came out of, I would have recognized the signs, but back in the '80s, there was no education or discussion about surviving physical and verbal abuse like there is now. However, when I was growing up in my aunt's house, I did witness some abuse. I mentioned earlier that I had just come out of an abusive relationship, but I would see my aunt and her husband start fighting after drinking on the weekends. We would be in our room, hearing everything, and the next day, everything would be fine. So let's just say that maybe I thought this was normal as well.

But I did meet this guy, and we became a couple. We never had any fights, and since I didn't know what verbal abuse was, it's possible there may have been some, but I thought it was okay. We also spent a lot of time downtown and were inseparable. We did many things together. I remember one time we were in the Head Shop, and he got into a fight with another guy. They were throwing punches, and I jumped into the fight too. I bit that man so hard that it drew blood, and I managed to get him off my man. People started calling us "Bonnie and Clyde." I loved him so much. I was still sixteen, and now I became pregnant with my first child. I remember feeling incredibly happy. I never thought I would get pregnant because in all those years with my first love, I didn't, but now it happened. I was living back at my aunt's place, and we had moved to another apartment area. He lived near me with his sister, and his parents also lived nearby. I met them, and from the beginning, I felt like a part of the family. They accepted me right away.

Doing my pregnancy, things were going well. My cousin would make sure I got to my doctor's appointments and took care of the necessary tasks during pregnancy. Having lived on the streets since I was twelve, I was accustomed to street life, but having a baby was a little scary. I didn't really know what to expect. I knew that life was going to be different, and one thing I knew for sure was that I didn't want my child to have the same life that I did. I wanted better, and I wanted the child to have a father involved in their life. I didn't have two pennies to rub together; I only had a couple of maternity dresses to wear. I would sit on the porch, and I remember a guy telling me one day that I looked like the Mona Lisa sitting there. But my thoughts were focused on the life I was about to bring into this world.

I always held my stomach and said, "This is a girl." I wanted my first child to be a girl. If I saw someone with beautiful hair, I would rub their hair and then rub my stomach, saying that I wanted my baby to have beautiful hair. Then the day came when the sonogram revealed that I was indeed having a girl. I was so excited. But I think I was living in a fantasy world. I believed that she would be like a baby doll, and all I had to do was dress her up in pretty clothes and put pretty bows in her hair. I bet girls at that age nowadays think the same way. They are in a fantasy, not realizing the challenges that come with providing clothes and financial support, especially if they don't have the father in their lives. But to top it off, on the day you give birth, babies come with tears, crying, sickness, and so forth. In my case, things were okay because my boyfriend was there for his baby. In fact, he was there for me too. I didn't know until later, but my mom had told him that he needed to give her money weekly for me when he got paid, so that I could buy things. I never saw the money, but he started giving it directly to me. I didn't have to worry too much when she was born because his family provided everything for me.

My cousin and his brother got together, and we came up with her name. In the South, it's common to have a nickname, so since she was born near Halloween, we decided to nickname her Pumpkin. On October 28, 1981, I gave birth to our first daughter. She was so beautiful with her lovely hair. My cousin was there with me throughout the whole process. Her dad was out of town working. When Pumpkin was born, she had two extra fingers that had to be removed. When she came home, she had every name brand item imaginable. His family spoiled her so much. He truly loved her. He would come to my house to see her and would just hold her and stare at her. He would always rub her stomach, which he called the alligator rub, and it would put her to sleep.

My mom used to say, "That man loves that baby. All he does is hold and stare at her." The fantasy world that I once lived in had now become a reality. Yes, I kept her dressed up and her hair done nicely, but girls, if you want to have a baby at a young age, it comes with a lot of work. Back then, we had to wash bottles and boil them to sterilize them. If you had a baby that stayed up all night crying, you would be tired the next day. I had a picture of Billy Dee Williams on the wall, and she would wake up in the middle of the night, and I would change her diaper and feed her while she would just stare at the picture. I remember one night saying, "Billy Dee, you have to go. My daughter has a crush on you." But babies are beautiful to have, but wait until you're ready.

Reality set in, as I mentioned. In fact, the day I brought her home, I was scared to death. You see, I had pictured her as a baby doll, but they don't come to life with movable arms and legs. They don't need bathing or their poopy diapers changed and so many other things that need to be done. As a matter of fact, a baby doll doesn't even have life because it's not real. But when you give birth to a baby, God gives it life, and it's up to us to be the mother and father we should be. It's a full-time, lifetime job.

The Enemy Tried to Kill Me: The Fight That Almost Took My Life

It was Christmastime, and during an argument, he swung at me, but I managed to duck. I saw the blood and remembered his previous threats on my life. I ran, trying to make it home as he chased me. I was severely beaten, with a black eye. I remember running toward a grassy field, fearing he would body slam me.

I was now seventeen, and our daughter was two months old. I was living with my cousin since things didn't work out well staying with my mom. He was living up the street at his sister's place. Things seemed to be going well. I loved being a mom and enjoy dressing up my baby. I would iron her little short sets and put her in bobby socks and tennis shoes. I believed we had a beautiful daughter, and I still do. He was playing the role of a dad, taking care of his baby, and there was nothing she lacked. If he couldn't provide something, I knew his family would. He had a sister in New York who would send boxes of things, and his other sister, with whom I was close, would spoil our daughter. Not to forget the grandparents, I had wonderful in-laws. Although we were never married, I referred to them as my in-laws, and I knew they saw me as their daughter-in-law.

Now, it's Christmas Eve, and he called me up, asking about going out. I agreed and started getting the baby ready for the night. We were laughing and talking on the phone, excited to go out and celebrate the holiday.

I got dressed and head up the street. We had just had a cheerful conversation on the phone, but when I arrived, everything changed. As we started talking, he became increasingly agitated and started talking nonsense and arguing. I didn't know who or what he was upset about. His anger escalated, and he tried to swing at me, but missed and ran into the wall, bumping his head. He then told me he was going to the bathroom and if he found his forehead bleeding, he would kill me. I had never seen him behave like this before, nor had I ever seen the look in his eyes. Knowing what I now know about domestic violence, I recognized these as signs of a Dr. Jekyll and Mr. Hyde personality. I was terrified and felt a fear I had never experienced before. I noticed the blood from his broken skin, and my instinct was to run, so I did. I ran behind the building, thinking it was the right moment to escape and make my way home, but it turned out to be the wrong time. He spotted me and started chasing after me. There was a man working on his car nearby, trying to help, but sometimes that can make the situation worse. My abuser began arguing with this man, accusing him of wanting me and saying all sorts of irrational things.

I took the opportunity to run, and I ran. Drawing from past experiences, I knew what it felt like to be slammed to the ground. As he chased after me again, I decided to head for a grassy area. However, he caught up to me there, and that was when he first physically assaulted me. I can still remember his fists landing blow after blow while I screamed and screamed. I don't even know how it eventually ended, but I managed to make it home. The next morning, which was Christmas, I sat on the edge of the bed, holding our two-month-old daughter, looking at her and crying, my black eye a painful reminder. While I had previously experienced being beaten up and left with black eyes by my first love, this time it was different—now I had a child with this man, the father of my daughter, and he was the one who had harmed me. It carried a different weight.

I walked into the kitchen where my family was sitting, and they looked at me, saying, "Girl, your eye is so messed up." It was so severe that I tried to cover it with sunglasses, but even they couldn't hide the extent of the injury. I didn't hear from him again until around New Year's Eve. He started calling me, apologizing and saying he loved me. I craved love, and he had me hooked once more. That night, we made plans to go out. I encountered his father, who asked, "Girl, what happened to your eye?" I replied, "Oh, I just got stung by a bee. You know how we can fix things up." I met up with him, and we took the city bus downtown, where we rented a hotel room to celebrate the New Year. Looking back now, I realize my eye hadn't even fully healed. It was still bloodshot and red, yet he walked beside me as if nothing had happened. People were looking at me, but it didn't seem to bother him at all. I suppose he knew I belonged to him, and deep down, I knew I wasn't going anywhere.

CHAPTER 2

The Enemy Called Low Self-Esteem

Have mercy upon me, O LORD; for I am weak:
O LORD, heal me; for my bones are vexed.
—Psalm 6:2

After enduring such a brutal beating by New Year's, I found myself back with him. I allowed him to do something that I had no right allowing. He whispered in my ear, and my already low self-esteem plummeted even further. I became incredibly weak in body, mind, and spirit, convinced that I didn't deserve any better.

In this chapter talk about the following:

- New Year's Eve we went to a hotel.
- I was wearing my funeral dress.
- Low self-esteem made me go back.
- He became even more controlling and possessive.
- There was a lot more fighting.
- I had now gotten pregnant with my son.
- He was all excited because he was having a son.
- Godmother's brother came into town.

- Godmother knew that I was living through pure hell.
- I went into labor with my son.
- I came home from the hospital, and everything was just so stressful.

The vicious cycle continued. My sister came to visit, and he despised her presence. Despite keeping the house spotless, he became furious when he saw boys at the table with my sister. A fight broke out, and the police were called. I remember finding refuge at someone else's house. My godmother came over, and we went to a skating party. He was infuriated that I took his son to the skating rink, and the abuse escalated even further. Another fight ensued, leading me to retreat to the back bedroom, desperately trying to reach for a knife. After that terrifying ordeal, I sought refuge at my uncle's house, and arrangements were made for me to catch a bus to Pennsylvania.

The New Year's Eve festivities were over, and we found ourselves back together. We decided it was time to get our own place. In the South, it's easy to find a furnished trailer, so that became our first home. It was a small and charming place. We settled in. Our daughter was now around four months old. A seventeen-year-old with a four-month-old baby, moving in with a twenty-seven-year-old man. Quite a situation! He went to work while I stayed home with our baby girl, who was the center of my world. I took great care in ironing her little shorts and putting on her cute white bobo sneakers. She had beautiful hair, and I loved braiding it. However, my cooking skills were lacking, and my attempt at making spaghetti was a disaster. I simply boiled the noodles and poured the sauce on top without properly mixing it, resulting in a sticky mess.

As time went by, I gradually learned how to cook with a few tips from his mother. Initially, living together wasn't too bad, but soon the fights started. I think I moved back home to my mom's place a few times. On one occasion, he came to my mom's house and began cursing and threatening us, insisting I return to him. My cousin stepped in and confronted him, leading to a chaotic situation. She walked away, and he went after me. She turned back to intervene, and he ended up punching her. Shortly after that night, I found myself back with him, attempting to shield my family from getting hurt or involved. He relished having me all to himself. Eventually, he became increasingly controlling and possessive. He didn't approve of me wearing makeup, and he would complain about certain clothes. I had one particular dress that I called my funeral dress because I only wore it to a funeral with my cousin.

We went to a club one night, and he saw some females he knew and started talking to them. I happened to see a guy from school and he came over to greet me. Oh my God, that was a big mistake. No other man was allowed to talk to me. He approached the guy, saying, "Man, what are you doing talking to my woman?" The guy explained that he knew me from school and just wanted to say hello. He cursed the guy out and before I knew it, he hit me. I'll never forget it. We were in the parking lot of the club, and he beat me up while people just seemed to be standing around.

There was a man with one arm there, and I overheard him saying, "Man, he's whooping her, but the more he knocks her down, she jumps back on her feet." At the time, I didn't fully grasp what he meant, but looking back, I realize that you can't keep someone down who doesn't want to stay down. When people try to hold you down, no matter how difficult or painful it may be, always find the strength to get back up. Eventually, he stopped and told me to come along because we were going home. I remember feeling so embarrassed. People were saying things like, "Wow, that's a shame," or "Man, he really beat her up," while others stared at me. I felt belittled. Since we didn't have a car, we had to walk home, and he continued to curse me out, calling me all kinds of names, all because I talked to a guy I knew from school. It was a way to tear down my self-esteem through verbal abuse.

As time passed, I became truly scared of him. I mentioned the Dr. Jekyll and Mr. Hyde personality earlier, and I can tell you he had it bad. He could be incredibly sweet, but it seemed like a couple of drinks would bring out a whole different person. His family believed that something must have happened when he was in the army. They said he used to be the sweetest boy, reminding me of our son whom I will speak of later, but when he returned from the army, he was a completely different person. Earlier, I mentioned a friend of mine whom I used to share clothes with, and she was sickly. Well, she ended up passing away a few days before turning 16. I was devastated. I didn't see all of them like I used to because we all went our separate ways, but she was like a sister to me. She died so young, and I often thought that she must have lived life to the fullest at a young age because she knew she didn't have much time left. I didn't get to attend her funeral because he caused such an argument, and I was scared, so I didn't go. I heard that all of our crew was there except for me. I cried and cried.

Time passed, and I was still with him, and now I was pregnant with our second child. I was 18 years old, and I found out that I was having a boy. Oh, man, he was excited about our pumpkin, but he was especially thrilled to be having a son. He said his nickname would be after his own nickname, Pong. Throughout the entire nine months of my pregnancy, there were no fights or many arguments. In fact, he made sure that I did everything right. I was also excited because I wanted my second child to be a boy. We had moved into an apartment, which happened to be in the same housing area where my godparents lived. I had met them when my pumpkin was born, and they were the sweetest people ever. They loved me as if I were their own. However, he didn't care for them too much because anyone I was close to, he didn't like, as it took me away from him. Nevertheless, we moved into the same housing area as my godparents. I was in my ninth month of pregnancy with our son, and on February 4, I gave birth to our handsome son, Pong.

On that morning, I woke up knowing that I was in labor. We had received a $400 check that day, and we wanted to spend the money. He told me to let him know whenever I was ready to go to the hospital. We cashed our check and were spending the money. I was craving Suzy Q's and Snickers. We went to his mother's house, and she said, "Vanessa, you are in labor," and I replied, "Yes, Mama, but I'm not ready to go." There wasn't much pain at all. I was also craving Vick's Drive-In fried chicken and rice with gravy. Anyone who knows Vicks Drive-In knows that they have the best soul food. So we went to get that for me to eat.

Around 11 o'clock that night, the pain began to worsen, and I told him we would be going to the hospital soon. And we did. He picked me up and carried me down the steps from the apartment to the car and drove me to the hospital. We arrived there at midnight, and seven minutes later, I gave birth to our son, Pong. The medical staff was upset that I had waited so long and that they had to rush to get me ready because my son was coming. It was an easy birth, and he was so handsome. His dad was incredibly proud. The next day, he brought his friends to the hospital and handed out cigars because he now had a son whose nickname was after his own. I came home on the third day, and oh my, it was a headache. He had been drunk since I had our son, celebrating, but now the baby was home, and I needed help. However, he was too busy partying and getting drunk.

There was an argument that started from the day I got home. It could be over anything. I still don't know how I made it. Now I have two beautiful children. I didn't work, but he did. I used to love the mornings of getting my little angels up, dressing them, cleaning the house, and hanging out clothes. Then I would have dinner fixed for when he got home. My godmother had three children of her own, and one day she said, "Hey, do you want to go with me to take the kids skating?" My son was around two or three months old, and my daughter was a year or two. I said, "Okay." I did everything I had to do around the house because everything always had to be spotless when he got home. So we left. It was a nice day, watching my god sister and god brothers skate. Then we left to come home, and when I got there, we all went into the house.

My children's father had gotten off work and was home by then. I was excited to see him and tell him what a nice time we had, but he snapped. He said, "What the hell are you doing taking my kids to a dusty skating rink? My kids don't need to be in a place like that." I went to say, "What's wrong with that?" and the fight began. He slapped me, and we went at it. My godmother was trying to break it up. Then he turned to attack her, screaming, calling her names, and saying he didn't like her anyway. The fight ended up in the bedroom. There was a pocket knife laying on the dresser, and I saw him cutting his eyes at it. I knew he wanted that knife. Somehow we were pushing and shoving each other, but I got to the dresser and I took my hand and pushed everything off so that he couldn't get to the knife.

The cops ended up coming. He didn't get arrested as I didn't press charges, nor did my godmother. I grabbed some things for myself and the kids and went to my godmother's house. I stayed there for a few days. Then came the honeymoon stage. This is one of the cycles you go through as a victim. It's the cycle where they sweet-talk you into believing that they really didn't mean it, that they love you, and that they will never do it again. They may even buy you gifts or take you out to dinner, etc. We believe it, fall for it, then go back, and everything is fine for a while until it starts all over again. So now I'm in the honeymoon stage. I go back.

Everything was going fine. In the first part of my story, I mentioned that I had a younger sister who is three years younger than me. I also mentioned how our lifestyle wasn't the greatest when I was at home. I made myself a promise that if I ever got my own place, I wanted her to move in with me. I talked it over with him, and it was okay. My sister moved in. She may have been in the tenth grade or so. Everything was okay; I loved having her there. I would wash her clothes and cook for her, just as I did for us and the kids. She was going to school and doing well.

Then one day she came home from school and asked if a couple of friends could come over to study. I told her yes, and he was at work, so I thought it would be okay. They were just kids studying. Oh my God, he came home. They were sitting at the kitchen table, and I was doing something in the kitchen while our kids were in the living room. He snapped, "What the hell are these niggas doing sitting in my house in my chairs? Get the hell out of here." They were just young school kids, and he acted like such a fool. They left, and he began cursing me out, saying that I do too much for her as it is, like washing her clothes and taking care of her as if she were one of my own kids. This argument went on for hours. My sister took the kids, and they were in the bedroom.

Later that evening, it got worse, and he jumped on me, beating me up. My sister grabbed the kids, and we ran to get help. We ended up at someone's house, and this time I called the cops. I was sick of it now. The cops came, and I told them I wanted to get some of my things and leave. They escorted me to the house and talked to him. They told him that I didn't press charges but wanted to get some of my things and the kids. My sister was also able to get some of her things. The cops waited while this took place. Then they took me to my uncle's house, who lived way out in the country. We contacted my brother, who lived in Pennsylvania.

We stayed at my uncle's for about a month. I knew he didn't know where I was at; he never knew about my uncle. I was really becoming more fearful of him now. I was on welfare, and back in those days, your check came in the mail. I outsmarted him. I knew that he knew what day was check day, so I went to the post office and explained what had happened and asked if they could keep my check and food stamps there, and I would pick them up. They did just that. He never got to me. My sister and the kids had bus tickets from the Greyhound bus station, and we were leaving for Pennsylvania. I had the cops escort me another time to the house to get more of our belongings before we moved to Pennsylvania.

A lesson to learn: if you ever need to go to your house for belongings, always take someone with you, or better still, take the law. It's very dangerous to go alone; they are still sometimes upset, and seeing you taking more things out could be dangerous. When I got to the house, we went in, and he was sitting in a chair playing "A House Is Not a Home" by Luther Vandross. Maybe he was hurting, maybe he was missing his family, but maybe if they feel like this, they should take a look in the mirror and want to change and seek help. We are on our way now to another state.

CHAPTER 3

Mind Games–The Abuser's Game of Choice

For thy mouth uttered thine iniquity and
thou chooses the tongue of the crafty.

—Job 15:5

I was on my way to Pennsylvania for a fresh start. On Father's Day, I called him, and this was a turning point. I let him into my ear, and because of this, I was just as good as back on the bus heading down south. His mouth uttered lies, and he was crafty. I fell for every word, hook, line, and sinker. The spirit of discernment is critical. For those of you who are reading and facing the exact same predicament that I faced, I am begging you to please seek God and His Holy Spirit, which will lead you into all truth.

In this chapter, I talk about the following:

- I stayed in Pennsylvania for one year.
- He would call during this time.
- He was even controlling over the phone.

- If the phone rang too long, he would get upset.
- I was still dealing with self-esteem issues, mind games, and his control.
- I had many friends and was still partying.

Beaver Falls, Pennsylvania. Back in the late '70s and early '80s, I thought this place was all that. When I was around eleven years old, my brother had sent for me and my sister to come up for the summer. Never having been out of Fayetteville, this was great. We arrived in the summer, and I tell you, I thought everyone up here was rich. Now, let's think—I am talking about two young girls who had never been anywhere and were never allowed to play with other kids. We didn't have much. My brother and his wife had a beautiful house. The people here were always dressed nicely, with their hair done up nicely, and I had an aunt who lived here who was always sharp. I used to say, "When I grow up, I want to be just like her." It just seemed like everyone was rich.

My brother and his wife took us shopping, and we got so many new clothes and shoes. Wow, we were two excited little girls. We had a lot of cousins up here whom we had never met, and we all just clicked from the beginning. Oh, it was so much fun. We had so many friends, and we would go down to the playground in the project and watch the guys play basketball, and we would do little cheers. We were finally having fun like kids would. When it was time to go back home, I would cry. I didn't want to leave all of that. I don't think we made it back up here until the year 1984.

My sister and I arrived in Pennsylvania the weekend of Mother's Day. My brother had gotten us an apartment. He and his wife had it all furnished, and everything we needed was in the apartment. They were excited, and so was I because I was starting all over. My son was just three months old, and my daughter was two and a half. My sister got signed up for school, and we were on our way to a new start. Now, everyone that I had known back in the day, we all had gotten older. I was the only one with kids. I was nineteen and had my own place. So you know, the hangout was at my place. We all reunited. It was nice. I was on my own, making my own decisions.

Well, I arrived here on Mother's Day weekend, and by Father's Day, I finally picked up the telephone to call him. Remember, he hadn't heard from me since the cops escorted us from the apartment. Yes, on Father's Day, I was calling him because I felt sorry for him. I felt that it was Father's Day, and he should hear from his children. You know, we often think more about them than we think about ourselves. Now he knows where I am, and this was the worst thing I could have done because now that I've gained a little strength and freedom, I have let him back into my ear. It's the worst thing we can do. We still have feelings for them, and they are cunning, knowing exactly what to say to pull us back in. Space is so needed if you are truly serious about leaving this relationship. And if kids are involved, ladies, be strong enough to talk about the children, but cut it short with anything else. Think about how you would expect them to think. Remember the lies they said before to lure you back in. Many women fall for the lie, even when their bruises speak the truth.

I moved back to North Carolina and fell for the lie. It felt like living in a fool's paradise. He promised not to hit me again. At that time, I was nineteen and he was twenty-nine. I went back to school and obtained my GED/HS diploma. I got my very first job. He worked in construction and was a good provider. Despite being abused, I hid the abuse. He told me he would quit drinking, but when I asked about it, he sarcastically replied, "You thought I would stop drinking for you." He was unpredictable and even threatened to blow up the hospital where I worked.

He would call me constantly. In the '80s, the telephone company did not provide call waiting, so if he called and the line was busy, he would become angry. Despite living miles away, he still controlled my telephone. He would send money weekly for the kids, thinking it would allow him to maintain control over me. Nevertheless, I continued to live my life here and formed a close bond with a family who lived behind me. The woman became like a mother to me. My kids and I would visit their house frequently.

During the daytime, I would hang out with people my age, and at night, I would socialize with the older crowd. My house became a popular hangout spot. In this town, people were friendly, and it seemed like everyone loved to party. There was a club called the ELKS, and it was the go-to spot. Even though I was only nineteen, I always managed to get into the clubs. I would hang out with the woman who was like a mother figure to me. Her kids or her niece would come and watch my kids while we went out. I would prepare dinner, feed the kids, give them hot baths, and put them to bed. By midnight, it was time to go to the ELKS. I loved to party. I wasn't much of a dancer, but I stayed on the dance floor. We would party all night, and when the lights came on signaling the end of the night, I would be disappointed because it meant it was time to go home. I was just enjoying myself and finally experiencing the freedom to go out, have friends, and have fun without being cursed at or beaten for trivial reasons. I felt free, like a bird released from a cage, making my own decisions.

I wasn't in a relationship with an older guy up here, can you believe that? Instead, I was dating a guy who was a year younger than me. I had known him since the summer we came up here. During that summer, he was like my first crush. You know how it is when we're kids. We were the perfect little couple. He had a ten-speed bike with *CC* as his initials and *VF* on the back. In the evenings, all of us kids would hang out on the blacktop, do cheers, and play games. The most that ever happened between us at that time was trying to kiss and grind on each other, not knowing what we were really doing. But we called ourselves crazy about each other.

As I mentioned before, when it was time for my sister and me to go back to Fayetteville, we would cry. And that was another reason I would cry, because I had to leave my first little crush. We kept in touch for a short time by writing letters to each other, and our letters would often end with a song, like the Commodores' "Three Times a Lady." So when I moved here in 1984, I saw him again. We hadn't seen each other since we were kids. And so he and I started dating. He was around eighteen, and we were quite different in many ways. I had two children and much more life experience. But it was okay. He adored my kids—well, everyone did. My friends who came to the house just spoiled them. I guess dating him gave me a taste of dating someone my own age. He was the only guy who held a special place in my heart at that time. I was simply enjoying life.

I lived a carefree life for over a year until the children's father whispered in my ears with apologies and declarations of love. He wanted his family back. He couldn't bear the fact that we were so many miles away. He claimed he couldn't make it without us, and I heard all these things before, but back then, I wasn't wise enough to realize they were empty words. He also promised that if I came back to him, he would quit drinking and never hit me again. Why do we allow ourselves to believe them? Yet we do, sometimes more than once. And then it becomes what I called it before—a honeymoon stage. I found myself at the beginning of my honeymoon stage once again.

Oh, he had my mind so tangled up with promises that this time we were going to make it. He assured me, so I said yes, I would come home. I told my sister that I was moving back. I don't even remember how she made it back down south or who she went to live with, but I had given up on her. I had made all those promises to take care of her when I got older, and I did for a while. But then I turned on her for a man who was nothing more than the father of my kids, a man who beat and treated me like nothing. He was also the reason for moving to Pennsylvania in the first place because he hated her and wanted to harm me because of her presence there. I can't forget everything my brother and his wife had done. They went out of their way to find us a place, furnish it, and I'm sure it took a toll on their time and money. They never asked for a dime; they did it because I was their sister, because I was fleeing from an abusive and crazy relationship. And now I was going to tell them I was going back. We never stopped to think about what we put our loved ones through when they help us.

And so now I was on my way back to North Carolina. I remember the day he was supposed to come. His father was driving his truck all the way here to pick us up. His father loved his grandkids, and he didn't mind the drive. All my friends were sad to see me leave. They arrived in the afternoon. He was glad to see his children, and they were happy to see their dad. That night, the older crowd invited us to go out, and we did. When we returned to my apartment, I went to say goodbye to everyone because we were leaving early in the morning. I became very sad, and he noticed, growing a little upset. I went out into the hallway with my godmother, and I remember telling her that I wanted to go, but then I didn't. I believe a part of me knew that it wasn't going to be better, but the other part went along with it. She used to always tell me, "Vanessa, you are a grown woman." Her father used to tell her, "You can only be raised once in life, and after you are grown, a man cannot call himself trying to raise you as his child. He needs to love you as his woman or wife." She would say, "Don't be that man's child." And that's how it is in these relationships. They act as if we are their children, and they try to mold us into what they want us to be.

I sometimes think that I stayed a lot of time for my kids. I never knew my dad, and I didn't want them to experience that. Not realizing the things that you really put them through. The next morning, we were a happy little family on our way back to Carolina. He already lived there in a trailer, and that's where we lived. After being away from him for over a year or so, I did gain a little self-esteem. I remember a friend in Pennsylvania telling me never to let a man kill my dreams and self-esteem. That kind of stuck in my head. I wanted to do something for myself. The one thing I wanted to do was get my high school diploma, so I did. I found out about a program that offered an Adult High School program after completing a certain number of weeks of school, and I did just that. He was keeping up with his promise, and things were going well.

I completed school, and we had a ceremony and all. I wore a black cap and gown and walked across the stage. I was so proud of myself. I set out to accomplish something for me, and I did. Then, I wanted to get a job, and I did. My cousin worked at the hospital and told me to apply. I was twenty and got my first job working in dietary. I was excited about my first job too. We had to wear white uniforms and white shoes. I always wore my little white dress, white stockings, and shoes. I thought it was so cute to be in uniform. As I said before, things were looking good. He did a lot of construction work, and now I was working.

Do you remember what he promised me to move back with him? Well, I had to work weekends, and one day after work, I came home to find him drunk as a skunk on the front porch. The kids were in the yard playing, and a friend of his came over, and they were drinking. I was so hurt. I said to him, "I thought you said you weren't going to drink anymore," and he replied, "Do you really think I'm going to quit drinking for you? Who are you? Who do you think you are?" I was devastated. That same night, not only was he drunk, but he also beat me up. The cycle repeated itself all over again.

Working at the hospital was great. We were like a family. I met a few friends, and we were close. There was one friend that he really didn't care for. It seemed as if he chose who he wanted me to be around. My one friend was tall with long hair, and the guys always seemed to be attracted to her. This friend he didn't like. He felt that if I was around her, it would bring attention to me. I had two other girlfriends, and we became close. We were truly like sisters.

My shifts were from 6:00 to 2:30 and 4:00 to 7:00 pm. At the time, I didn't drive, so he had to pick me up for work. Working in dietary, I sometimes had to prepare desserts for the next day or next shift. One day I was assigned to dessert, and as a newcomer, I had some difficulty cutting up the dessert to put in the bowls, which caused me to be a few minutes late punching out. Well, this didn't sit well with him. He went off on me. When I got in that car, he cussed me out so badly because I was late. I tried to explain, but he didn't want to listen. He even made threats, saying he would blow up the hospital. I was so afraid of him, especially the way his voice sounded. I genuinely thought he might actually carry out his threat. My coworkers never knew that some days when I came to work, I may have been up half the night dealing with his rage.

There were a couple of guys who worked with us and were great friends to me. Have you ever known someone who was drop-dead gorgeous and everyone loved and adored? Well, that's how they were. They made me feel special. I guess what I'm saying is that I put him on a pedestal, and when you're up there, you never think that person would come down to your level. But they did. They were my friends. On days when I was feeling down or had a bad night at home, just having them treat me like I was equal to them made me feel good. You never know whose life you touch. You never know what a person may have just gone through the night before, which is why it's so important to treat everyone with kindness and show them love. Instead of talking about them or laughing at them, reach out to them. You never know, you could be the light on someone's darkest day.

There were a lot of dark days for me. When they say we can cover it up well, I guess it's true. And once again, back in those days, you didn't hear about domestic violence as much as you do today. I did write to my godmother in Pennsylvania. I wrote her a ten-page letter expressing how hurt I was that I gave up everything to come back to this man who lied to me. He was doing the same thing. I was hurt. Of course, I continued to live with him, and we applied for an apartment in Colonial Place. One day the mail brought us news that I had been approved for an apartment. We were so excited. These are nice apartments located in the complex where his family and my family lived. We were moving out of the trailer and into an apartment.

The Vicious Cycle Repeated Itself

I am come a light into the world, that whosoever
believeth on me should not abide in darkness.
                                             —John 12:46

In 1988–1989, crack cocaine emerged on the scene, and it became a part of my life. While still raising my kids, I continued to make dinner and keep my house clean, and I still went to work. I was what you would call a functional user. My life was incredibly chaotic, and I couldn't distinguish up from down. I was living in complete darkness, hiding behind a mask that blocked out any light and kept all the darkness trapped inside.

In this chapter talk about the following:

- I was self-medicating with the drugs and the alcohol.
- Through everything, God still had his hands on me.
- Older brother introduced me to drugs.
- I was living in this functional, crazy abuse; my life was so out of order.

In 1987, we moved into Colonial Place, where our first child was born. We had family members living in the area, including his mother, sister, and my cousins. Despite the ongoing abuse, it seemed like we were making progress. We rented a three-bedroom apartment. I continued working at the hospital, and he was still involved in bricklaying and construction work. Our children were growing up—our daughter was in second or third grade, and our son was attending Head Start. Soon after settling into our new apartment, my oldest brother came to town. I hadn't seen him since we left Pennsylvania, so I was excited. He asked if he could stay with us, and we both agreed. I cherished the opportunity to have a relationship with all of my siblings, just like in the books I used to read, such as *The Boxcar Children* and *The Brady Bunch*. My brother moved in, and both he and my husband were skilled card players. We would occasionally have card games on weekends, which was a lot of fun. They would invite friends over, and after bathing and putting the kids to bed, the games would begin. If my husband didn't win, my brother often would. One night, my brother had such a winning streak that he earned enough money to buy a used car.

As always, things would be going well, and then something would trigger an argument. There was a guy whom my husband had apparently cheated out of some money, and they had a heated argument. The guy told my husband it wasn't over. One day, my husband came home from work early, with a messed-up eye. The guy had attacked him in the parking lot. He walked into the house, and I pretended to feel sorry, but deep down, I couldn't help but think, *Good, now you know how it feels.* His eye was swollen for a few days. This incident put an end to our card games because my husband was now determined to seek revenge. And when he said revenge, he meant it. One day, he came home early from work while the children were at school. He had a crazed and angry look on his face. He said, "Come on with me." We left the house and walked up to his mother's house. He broke the lock on a window and told me to crawl through it and unlock the front door. I was terrified. I went in and unlocked the door, and he followed. His father had some hunting rifles, but my husband had something else in mind on that particular day. He wanted to confront the guy who had beaten him up. I was filled with fear. He grabbed the rifle and said, "Let's go."

We began walking toward the building where the guy lived. My husband instructed me to go up and knock on the door, asking for the guy. I was already filled with fear, seeing the rage in him and being terrified of guns, but I was too afraid to refuse. This is the dynamic that exists in some of these relationships. We are so mentally controlled and scared of them that we do whatever they tell us out of fear of being beaten up. So I did it. I went and knocked on the door, asking for the guy, but instead, his brother approached the door, and then I heard a gunshot. I think I have never run so fast in my life, screaming all the way back to the house. Thankfully, his aim was off because someone could have been seriously injured.

Not long after that incident, my uncle came to town. We hadn't seen him in years. He was a truck driver and happened to be in his old hometown of Fayetteville. He came to my house, and we decided to have a small house party, something we did from time to time. After putting the kids to bed, we would move the coffee table out of the way, drink, play music, and dance. So, when my uncle arrived, it was time to celebrate. His sister, nephew, and a friend joined us. My brother and uncle were reminiscing, laughing, and talking about old times, while the rest of us enjoyed the music, drinks, and dancing. As the night grew late, the party started winding down. After our guests left, my uncle went to lie down, and we began tidying up.

An argument erupted for some reason, and the yelling and screaming intensified. He grabbed me and threw me across the room onto the couch. My brother was furious. He swung at my husband, warning him never to hit me again. Then he stormed out of the house. My children's father was livid. He told his nephew to come along, declaring that they were going to confront my brother for hitting him. He retrieved an old rusted sword that he kept in the car. As my brother was returning across the street, my husband went after him. He swung the sword, grazing my brother's back, and then swung again, narrowly missing his nose. My brother managed to escape, rushing back into the house, where he yelled, screamed, and cursed at me. It was a long, tumultuous night before things finally settled down.

The next morning, it was as if nothing had ever happened. There were times when you never knew what might set him off. It had gotten so bad that I could sense when something was about to happen. Victims can wear the mask of normalcy well. We cover up so much. I was taking care of the children, going to work, and most people never knew what I was going through. That part we keep hushed and silent. I believe we gather strength to endure all that we go through. Our lives become programmed. I knew I had to keep my house spotless, not that I didn't already, but this was what he expected. I knew he had served in the army for a short time, and he would talk about how the sergeant would enter their rooms and flick a quarter onto their beds. If it didn't land a certain way, he would tear the bed apart, and they would have to make it all over again.

Sometimes I think a lot of his controlling behavior stemmed from his time in the army. I had to have his dinner prepared at a specific time. He wanted it to be hot when he came home from work, which is when we would have dinner. There's nothing inherently wrong with a woman waiting on her partner, but it shouldn't be a chore. Waiting on him became burdensome. I would fix his meals and bring them to him, along with a cold drink, according to his preferred timing. I mean, this was when he wanted it. I was just as tired as he was, taking care of small kids and going to work. As I mentioned, there's nothing wrong with taking care of each other, but it shouldn't be an expectation placed solely on you. It made me feel like his child. He would dictate who my friends and family could be and tell me what to wear and what not to wear. If his food wasn't cooked a certain way, he would explode.

One day, I made steaks and I overcooked his. He called me into the kitchen and said, "What in the hell is this? This is not how my steak should be." You want to talk about verbal abuse. He cursed me out so badly. I remember being mad and upset, and I saw a butcher knife on the counter. He noticed me looking at it and said, "What, you want to kill me? Here, take the knife." He slapped me and said, "Fix me a beer." He went into the living room and sat down. I was crying and fixing him a cold glass of beer. As I was preparing the beer, I saw a can of roach spray. I thought to myself, "I'm going to poison him today." I sprayed the roach spray into his beer, cleaned around the rim of the glass, and took it to him. I sat down, terrified of what might happen. I was scared that if it killed him, I would go to jail; and if he found out what I did, he would kill me. Thank God he just went to sleep.

There were many times when I would think about how I could escape from this crazy life. It seemed like it was getting worse. He was drinking even more. It had gotten to the point where he would carry around a bag and always keep a pint of wine in it. I never understood why. I didn't drive at that time, but he felt it was time for me to learn. So he began to teach me how to drive. Even though I drank, I was more in control of myself than he was, so he taught me to drive. He was actually a good teacher. I remember one night when it was just him and me, and I could see, but not very well. He let me drive a few miles without realizing that he had turned the lights off. Sometimes when we were driving, he would say, "Stop," and I would stop abruptly. He said it was his way of teaching me to be ready for anything that might happen. But I got my driver's license when I was around twenty-one years old.

One Issue After the Next

For where envying and strife is, there is
confusion and every evil work.

—James 3:16

The Word of God states that He will not give me more than I can bear, but this was a bit much. There was strife, confusion, and contention at every turn. There was always something going on, always an issue, always a fight, and the police were always being called. Living like this was taking a toll on me. Looking back at all of this, I can see that I am only here by the grace of God, His unmerited favor.

In this chapter, I talk about the following:

- Every holiday there was a fight; there was always confusion.
- God is not the author of confusion.
- Uncle came to visit.
- There was a card party going on that resulted in an altercation.

On the streets, it was always an eye for an eye. My children's father got beat up, and he sought revenge on the person who had attacked him. He broke into his mom's house to get a hunting rifle. I was afraid because I knew how unstable he was. He went after the person, and I was unknowingly made an accessory to his crime. He went to jail and eventually got out.

The issues continued. In 1988-1989, we moved into a drug-infested apartment. My sister was pregnant, and our family came down for Christmas. We decorated the house, but something didn't feel right. He was acting unusually nice, which was strange because he was usually a troublemaker. My son was playing with my sister's husband, and this made him jealous. A fight broke out, and he grabbed a meat cleaver. My daughter started screaming, "No, daddy, no!" The cops came and took him to jail.

In 1988, we had been discussing moving from Colonial Place. The area was changing, and after the fight incident, things felt different. I had signed up for an apartment in Rosemary, which was through the housing authority. I remember the day we found out we were going to move. We were both so excited, as were the kids. We were now moving over to Murchison Road, or as locals call it, the "Merk"! Moving to the Merk meant being in a busy area with many clubs and hole-in-the-wall type places. It was known for being a rough area. When we moved in, crack cocaine had just hit the city. We were introduced to snorting cocaine when a family member visited town. Personally, it wasn't something I cared for, but I still did it from time to time.

Once we were all settled in, our place looked cute. I remember our living room had blue furniture and light blue curtains. My daughter's room was decorated with a Strawberry Shortcake theme, while my son's room had a sports design and was painted all blue. It felt like home. We had good neighbors—a family lived to our left, and their little girl became friends with my daughter, while a family lived to our right, and their little boy became friends with my son. The four of them were friends. We still loved to party, and one of our neighbors did too. On Friday nights, my friend from the hospital would come over, and we would enjoy our favorite liquor and beer. We would all sit outside with the neighbors, the kids would play, and we would have music playing, having a good old time. We loved listening to old music. Sometimes our partying would end in a fight. I'm not sure what would set him off, but he would become enraged, cursing you out over trivial things. Even though we lived there, we gradually stopped taking the kids on rides and having picnics like we used to.

I remember times when I would gather my two kids and put them in the backseat of the car. We would go to the store and get them some treats, and then we would just go for a drive. However, there were also times when I would be driving and crying, and my son would say, "Don't worry, mommy, be happy." Kids have the ability to see and feel our pain. When we are in these types of relationships, we often fail to see and recognize what our children are going through because we are too focused on surviving for ourselves and for them. But it does have an impact on the child. They may be little people, but they have the same five senses as we do.

Now, as I mentioned earlier, I learned how to drive, and now I was driving him around a lot because his drinking was getting worse. Things had worked out between him and my brother, and my brother had moved back in with us. In 1988, crack cocaine had arrived in town. Many people were now smoking it and becoming addicted.

Additionally, this was around the time when AIDS emerged. It seemed like 1988 and 1989 were difficult years for my age group, as several friends died during that time from AIDS, overdoses, or other causes. I remember having a conversation with an old school friend, and we expressed how scary it was that so many of the people we grew up with in Cross Court were experiencing these problems. But crack cocaine had a profound effect on individuals back then, and it also became a part of our lives. We started smoking crack. We would take a beer can or a soda can, flatten it in the center, punch some small holes in it, and sprinkle cigarette ash on the holes. This is where we would place our piece of crack. Then, we would light it with a lighter and start smoking through the open hole. Crack cocaine had a strong allure once you started. It seemed like people were stealing or selling crack everywhere. The nice place we lived in had now become a popular spot for selling drugs.

There are two types of addiction: functional and non-functional. We were functional because we could still manage our daily lives, taking care of the kids, working eight-hour days, and partying all night. Looking back, I wonder how I was able to do it. Sometimes we would smoke crack all night, then I would take a shower around 5 a.m. and go to work at 6. I would sometimes be high as a kite. By 2:30 p.m., I would finish work, pick up the children, and go home to do my duties. Well, not really my duties, but remember the house had to be spotless. Dinner had to be cooked and ready to be served when he got home. Also, depending on where he worked, I would have already gone to see him. If I was on the telephone when he tried to call and couldn't get through (remember from the previous chapter that this made him mad), it was not a good situation. He always needed to know who, what, and when. When the Bell Atlantic Telephone Company introduced three-way calling, I was like a kid with a new toy. I could talk to whomever I wanted, stay on the phone as long as I wanted, and he would never know. The crack was becoming more and more entwined in our lives.

There was a time when I had to get a wisdom tooth pulled. I came home from work to go to the dentist, and he was at home with crack. We started smoking. When I got to the dentist, I was so high that they didn't even need to medicate me, but of course, I didn't tell them. We came home and continued to get high. My mouth was numb, and I was trying to smoke. It was crazy! By then, we had moved away from using cans and started using little stems (pipes). Imagine having a numb mouth and trying to smoke from a pipe. That's how crack had a grip on us. Many people would do anything just to get another hit. They called it "femming" for another hit. I thank God that it didn't consume me entirely. You would see people do almost anything just to get a small piece, just enough to make them crave more. We would pay around $20 for a rock. Drug dealers were getting rich while people were becoming addicted and not only dying physically but also mentally. Some of the places where you could buy crack were dangerous. There would be guys standing around with guns at certain spots. It was wild. Even the apartment area we had moved into, which we initially thought was nice, had now become an area where drugs were widely sold. There would be a few guys standing on the corner at specific spots, waiting for someone to stop and pick something up.

When we lived there, all of this was happening, but it never really stood out to us. I guess because we had always been part of the street life, these things didn't matter to us. Our children never knew what we were doing because we took care of them and kept our activities separate. Sometimes, my cousin, who spoils all the kids in the family, would come and take them for the weekend. I remember a few times we even thought about buying crack and cooking it ourselves to sell. A friend of ours who lived next door gave him an eight ball. He was supposed to cook it up and sell it, splitting the money with our friend. Well, that never happened because he cooked it, and we smoked it. We were scared, thinking this guy was going to be furious. Thankfully, he was a close friend, and we were able to work something out with him. Even with all of this going on, it didn't stop the arguing and fighting.

My children and my brother tell me that there were many times when he would act out, and we would leave. Some things I guess I blocked out and don't remember, but I do recall some nights when I found myself grabbing the kids and calling my cousin or someone to come and get us, and they would, but the next day we would go right back. I was always scared to call the cops because he would say, "Call the cops, and I will kill you before they get here." He was getting worse. To this day, I still don't know what was wrong with him. I mean, we had some good days. He loved his children. He would come home from work and always have candy or something for them. We would have picnics and do family activities, but if he had alcohol in him, he would change. The littlest things would set him off. It was like walking on eggshells. One night, we got into a fight, and I grabbed the kids and started walking. The guys who were standing on the corner asked me what was wrong. I was scared because I thought if he saw this, he would really lose it. Then he showed up, and those guys confronted him, saying, "You better never hit her again, or we will beat you to death." One of the guys took us to the neighbor's house, which was his mom's, and we stayed there for a while. I guess those guys put some fear in him because when I got home, he was asleep. Thank God. The worst that could have happened that year was during Christmastime. We were so happy. Our kids always had a nice Christmas, but for some reason, this Christmas felt even more special. I had decorated the house, and the kids were excited. Little did they know that everything they had asked for, they would receive on Christmas morning.

My oldest brother was living with us, and I got a surprise that my baby brother was coming in from Pennsylvania. I had not seen him in years, and he had never met or knew him. Well, my brother was only here for a couple of days and was going back on Christmas Eve night. We were all enjoying the holiday. I was cooking, and the children were running around playing. We were drinking and having fun. It was Christmas Eve. I kept telling my oldest brother, "Something is going to happen. It feels too good. Oh, I just know something is going to happen." Well, my brother said his good-byes and headed back to Pennsylvania.

On Christmas morning, the kids woke up and ran downstairs. I can still see them jumping around and tearing up gifts. They were so happy. We both smiled as we watched them. Soon after all the gifts were opened, all the craziness began. I was finishing preparing Christmas dinner, and the kids were dressed and playing outside. He had left. I didn't know that he had gone to a friend's house and started trouble. It had something to do with money, and they owed it to him. He wanted his money. They wouldn't open the door, so he took a brick and threw it through the window.

The girl in the house was pregnant, and they were furious. They, of course, called the cops. He came back to the house, and I didn't know who in the world he was. He was like a madman. He was snapping out so badly. He would leave, and the cops would come to the house looking for him. Then he would come back, snapping out, and he would leave again. The cops were now calling, wanting to know if he had come back. It was crazy.

I had made this green sherbet punch for the kids, and every now and then, our kids would come in with some friends to get some punch. One time, our daughter was coming in with her friends at the same time that he was, and he was screaming and cursing. I remember saying, "Hey, don't you see these kids here?" And he said, "I don't give a care." The kids went back out the door, and he continued fussing. Then he left the house again.

This time, my sister, who is six months pregnant, and her husband stopped by to visit. My son had gotten a train set for Christmas, and it was set up for him by the Christmas tree. So while my sister and I were in the kitchen laughing and talking, her husband was in the living room playing with my son and the train set. All of a sudden, the front door swung open. Here comes my children's father. Remember, he really doesn't like my sister. He sees her husband playing with my son and says, "Who the hell told you to touch that train set? I bought that for my son. Who do you think you are coming in here touching my son's stuff?"

My sister and I go into the living room, and a big argument starts. He's cursing them out, telling them to get out of his house, and my sister is going back at him. Then I tell him to leave my sister alone. That's when he hits me, and things get crazy. My sister tells him to never hit her sister again, and he says, "You know what, I've got something for all of you." He goes into the kitchen. We have a closet where we keep the brooms and things, and he grabs a meat cleaver. He's now coming toward us. My sister, who is six months pregnant, is in front. I am behind her, and then her husband is behind me, along with my son. As he comes toward us with this meat cleaver, meanwhile, my pumpkin is coming through the back door, and she begins to scream, "Daddy, nooo!" We all end up in the front yard.

As we did, the cops were pulling up. Neighbors were all outside, my kids were crying, and their dad is getting arrested. They took him to jail. Christmas day, which had seemed to be so beautiful, turned out to be a disaster. My sister and her husband left. My cousin came by and took me and the kids with her. I had cooked a big old feast that was left for an empty house while we spent Christmas at the friends of my cousin whom we didn't even know. We were afraid that he would get right back out, and it would be a fight all over again. He used to scare me anyway because he would say, "I don't care if you call the cops, I will kill you before they get here," or he would say, "You can go get that PFA paper. I don't care about no paper. I will kill you before the cops get here." He did spend a couple of days in jail, and I told him that before he came back, he would have to get some help. It was getting to be too much. He said he would, and he did sign up at some alcoholic group.

I was happy, and of course, I believed him again that he was going to do this and get himself together. I really wanted this to happen. I had always wanted my kids to be raised up with their father, just something that I didn't have. They loved their dad. I mean, there were some good times. We would go to the park and have little picnics. When he would come home from work, he would bring them things, and they looked forward to dad coming home. Then there were those times that were just crazy. It would be like walking on eggshells. But he did do the group thing, just enough for me to take him back. And once again, I was made to look like the dumb one because he started all over again.

CHAPTER 6

Enough Is Enough

*I am weary with my groaning; all the night make I
my bed to swim; I water my couch with my tears.*
—Psalm 6:6

I was growing weary day by day; I could not continue living like this. Because of what I know now and my relationship with Christ Jesus, I know that it was Him who kept me even when I did not want to be kept, even when I was getting high on crack and drowning my sorrows in alcohol.

The kids were now five and seven. I was growing tired of this man, tired of everything. He was always controlling. My body was growing weary, and I was so sorrowful. Food had to be cooked right. I built up enough courage and asked him to leave. He took everything out of the apartment that he could sell. My son would sit and watch the spot where the TV once was. After nine and a half years of abuse, he was gone. We got a TV back and slowly got other things. He was still talking in my ear, trying to get me back.

Time had passed, and I had not heard from him. We are now in the year 1989.

Well, now we are into another year. As I said in the last chapter, I decided to give him another chance. So he does well for a while, and then it starts again. I can recall a time when we were having dinner, and both of us were sitting in the living room eating. He wanted the salt shaker or something, and I said something like, "Wow, I just sat down," and he got upset. Started cursing me out, so I got up to get it, and when I did, he got up behind me and kicked me straight in my behind. He was just so controlling. My brother was living with us again, and I would cook dinner, and my brother would be ready to eat, and I would say, "Oh no, we have to wait for him to come home," and I really did have to. I knew to have his food ready for him when he came in the door. The house had to be spotless. I was getting to the point where I was really getting tired of all of it.

Our children were getting older; now they were five and seven. I was tired of them seeing all the fighting and also grabbing them, leaving the house because of fighting. Even sometimes when we would go out to eat, he would act out. We went for dinner one night for pizza, and the waitress was taking so long, and when she did get there, he cursed her out. Then he started with me because I would say something. He just acted out whenever, wherever. Even when my family would try to come around, I was so afraid he was going to want to fight.

The Fourth of July came about, and my family wanted to come over. I used to make this punch with 150 proof grain alcohol in it. You would cut up fruits to go in it, and if you didn't watch how much you drank, it would knock you out. Well, this particular day, he had started wanting to act up. I made that punch, and he began to drink it. He drank so much, and I let him, also, that it knocked him out cold.

The family and I had a good old Fourth of July. We laughed, took pictures, and enjoyed ourselves. When he did wake up, everyone was gone, and he really didn't remember much of anything. I was happy; that was one holiday we got to enjoy. But that was how it was. As I was saying, I was getting tired of stuff. By now, we were more into smoking crack and still drinking. Even with that, I was getting tired. I think he could see that also. I would smoke, but it wasn't getting the best of me as it was him. I had finally gotten to the place where I wanted out. I had enough. We, as women, want to feel like we are loved, not by the hands of our man. We want to be told that we are pretty and that we look good by our man, not always put down and called names, made to feel like we are just there to take care of the kids and the house, and please them in bed when they want to be. If some of us are honest, we don't even enjoy it because you probably just got called names if not knocked out.

There comes a time in life when women get enough strength to say that they have had enough. This is also their most dangerous time. So I was tired of everything, and I told him he had to go. I couldn't believe it, but he said, "Fine, I'm out of here." He packed his stuff, and he also took all that he could take that he could pawn. He took the washer and dryer, microwave, television; he even took the telephone out of the wall. I really didn't care. I just wanted him out. Someone gave me a television for my son. He used to sit and just stare at the TV all the time. I didn't know then, but that was his escape, to just stare at the TV to block things out. Nevertheless, he was out of our house. Many times, he tried to come back. I think he tried everything. He called and said that he would change and things would be better. Nope, I didn't buy it. He signed himself up for a program where he could get help, and then he wanted me to bring the kids for him to see. Nope, it didn't work. I told him, "No, I am still not taking you back." I believe he had to stay in this place for a few weeks. He wanted me to help him find an apartment so that when he was released from this place, he would have somewhere to go. I said, "Nope." I guess he thought that I wouldn't survive without him.

The kids had started back to school when he wanted to see them, and I felt good because when he saw them, they were in new clothes, looking just as good as if he was there. This was good for me and good for women to see that we think that we cannot make it without them. That is why a lot of times women stay for the support, but as I found a way to take care of myself and my children, you can too. We can be independent and own our own. He did get out, and I don't know where he went to stay, but a few other times he did ask me to take him back. I remember one time he went and got a hotel room and had some alcohol and some cocaine, and he called me to come. He said, "I have all this stuff here, we can party." I was like, "Nope." So by now, he is getting upset because I'm still saying "Nope." I would stay sometimes at my apartment or with my cousin because they would help with the kids. So a few times he came over to the apartment complex looking for me. There was one time he had someone act like they wanted me to come out, but actually it was him. We found out that he was waiting on the side of the building with a brick in his hand, hoping that I would walk out. Another time he caught me as I was going to get in my car, and he snapped, cursing me out and wanting to fight. He was really upset because I meant that it was over, and I believe he knew this time I was for real, and I was. Enough was enough, and I have had enough.

CHAPTER 7

The Spirit of Murder Was in Me

*And the Lord said, Simon, Simon, behold, Satan hath
desired to have you, that he may sift you as wheat.*
—Luke 22:31

Many times in life, the past would always try to resurrect
itself. We have to know how to use wisdom and leave the
past in the past when it is warranted. My past came back, I
welcomed it, and it almost caused my life. The enemy did try
to sift me as wheat, but to God be the glory. God had a plan.

I saw my first love again and went with him. I got sick
three to four months later and was diagnosed with a tumor.
Surgery was scheduled for the following Monday. I went out
to party since I would be down for a while. I felt really weird
and was drinking a lot. It felt like I was being stalked.

In the face of death, my children's father and my first
boyfriend had a deadly meeting. He started chasing us, and
my first boyfriend ran. I ran to my room and fell into a fetal
position. He started beating me with a baseball bat. The beating went on for a long time. I was crying out to the neighbor for help. I began crying out to God. His bat was called
Freddy Krueger. He swung the bat and I looked at him and

said, "If you kill me, who is going to raise our children?" He told me to get up and wash the blood off my face.

The police showed up, and I ended up in the hospital. I was told that I would never walk again. Family came to see me, and the kids started screaming when they saw me. Pins were put in my body, and I also had four casts.

He turned himself in, and the kids were sent to Pennsylvania. With four casts on my body, I found myself in the crack house and drinking, still self-medicating. I went to the doctor to get the casts off. I was walking. It was indeed a miracle.

On December 5, I got on a bus to go to Pennsylvania. I wanted to surprise my kids. My brother picked me up, and the kids were happy to see me, and I was happy to see them. Went to see my godmother. My kids were different; it was as if they were restricted. Got an apartment, moved in, and only had food stamps. Had to pay my family back for everything that they had done to help me and the kids. I was still messed up in the head. I realized that through all the beatings, my tumor never burst.

As I said in the last chapter, my mind and my heart were made up that it was over. I had enough. For nine and a half years, I lived in verbal, mental, and physical abuse. Now, in spiritual terms, nine means birthing, that God will birth something in you and out of you. If anyone has ever had a baby, we know that birthing is painful. I look at things in my life now and in the spiritual terms of things I didn't know back then that there was a mandate on my life to reach hurting people who suffer through some of the same things that I had experienced. I had to go through a series of pain. When you are pregnant, those nine months are not always comfortable, and neither were the nine years I was in this relationship. At the nine-month mark, a woman gives birth, and those contractions are painful, something you don't want to endure, but you have to because you have to bring life to someone, whether it's a boy or girl. The same thing with my nine years, I was at the end, and I had to go through my pain to let someone else have life from what they have suffered through. And here comes the story of my pain.

Now he was a construction worker, and the company that he worked with would sometimes send him out of town for a few days. Well, I didn't hear from him for a while, so I thought that he was out of town.

Life went on for me. I was still trying to work and take care of the kids. I was living between my apartment and my cousin's. I was still partying and having a good time. Back then, I was a little wild, I guess you can say. One day, my cousin and I were out driving, and we started racing each other. Unfortunately, I ended up with a flat tire. I thought to myself, "Man, my tire is messed up, and I don't have any money." That day, I was working at the hospital, and guess who I ran into? My first love. Oh my God, I hadn't seen this man in years. He was at the hospital because he had gotten into a car accident and was there for a follow-up. I was like, "Wow." We started talking, and I told him about my tire situation. Coincidentally, he had just come into some money, and let's be real, if a man is going to spend some money, we're going to let him spend some money. So I did. He got me a new tire for my car, and we started reminiscing about old times. You can probably guess where things went from there. We decided to see each other again, and we did. We started hanging out, and things seemed great. However, I began to get sick, experiencing severe stomach pains. He took me to the doctor, and I was diagnosed with a tumor. It was a tumor that had actually grown like a baby, complete with hair and a tooth. I was told that I had to get it removed because if it were to burst, I would die. So my doctor scheduled surgery for the upcoming Monday. I thought to myself, *Okay, if I'm going to have surgery on Monday, then I need to get my party on because I'm going to be down for a few days or weeks.* So we decided that Friday night we were going to hit the town and go out to party. This would be the first time that we actually went out. Up until then, we had mostly just hung around the house after we both got off work, drinking and reminiscing about the old times.

One thing I distinctly remember is that he had a tattoo of my name on his arm. While he was in prison, he got it done. He would say that the inmates would say, "Man, that young girl must really mean something to you."

I sort of believe I did even though our relationship was crazy. When we were together, we cared for each other. He had always sent a message to the children's father that when he got out, he was getting his woman back.

Well, after seeing him and he fixed my tire, we decided to see each other again. Now, Friday is approaching, and I get my cousin to babysit the kids. It's payday and it's Friday. I'm off and rush home to get the kids' stuff together as well as my own. It's maybe around seven or so, and his brother comes to pick us up, and we head to my cousin's to drop off the kids. We're all in a good mood, you know, all ready to party. I get to my cousin's house, kiss the kids goodnight, and tell them I'll see them tomorrow. I get back in the car, and whoohoo, let's party. We've got the music blasting, and back then, we would drink in the cars as we ride, so we were passing the drinks. I don't remember what I was drinking, but it may have been E&J Brandy and Coke. That was my favorite back then.

So when I got in the car, I had a drink. Now, as I mentioned before, I was a drinker. I had been drinking since I was thirteen, and now I'm twenty-five, so I could handle my drinks. But we were pouring the drinks. We were maybe two or three blocks from my cousin's house when I spilled liquor all over myself, and I started feeling weird. I told them to take me to my other cousin's house where me and the kids some- times stayed. I had clothes there, and I wanted to change. Even though I was feeling funny, I was still drinking. We went there, and I remember all of us going into the house. I intro- duced them to my brother and told him what had happened and that I was changing clothes. After I finished changing, we were ready to leave. I remember telling my brother that we were going to the club and that we were going to get our party on. We left. When I spoke about feeling weird, well, I was still feeling that way. So much that I don't remember that night. I can recall being at this one club, but I don't even know when we got there. All that I remember is being in the back seat of the car, arguing with him, and him trying to get me out of the car, but I didn't want to.

Then the next thing I remember is being at another club. I don't even remember walking into that club, but we were on the dance floor, and he and I were arguing. I kept saying, "Take me home, I just want to go home." I don't remember much of that night, but I really believe he beat me up. The next thing I can recall is us stopping at a stop- light, and I looked up and saw my old neighbor. I blanked out, and the next thing I knew, we were at a gas station. I got out and used the phone booth to call my brother, but I don't remember what I said. After that, my memory is blank until about 4 o'clock in the morning. I was in my bed, and the guy I was with was shaking me to wake me up. He was saying, "Vanessa, wake up, someone is at your door." I got up, feeling extremely dizzy, and looked out the window. I remember saying, "Dag, what does he want?" I told him it was my kids' father. We both turned to go downstairs, and as we were going, I heard glass break. Before we could reach the bottom of the stairs, there was my kids' father. We both turned around and started running back up the stairs.

Ladies, remember when I said I would explain later about trust? Well, here it goes… The man who promised me that he had my back has now left me. He claimed that he got knocked out of the window. I'll never believe that. I believe he jumped out of that window, and the one he was supposed to be protecting was now facing death alone. I ran into my bedroom and closed the door, curling up in a fetal position. At that moment, my children's father came in behind me and began attacking me with a wooden baseball bat. I remained in that fetal position while he swung that bat like a madman. He beat me repeatedly, then he would go downstairs, and I could hear him smashing things with the bat. He would come back upstairs and resume beating me. At one point when he ran downstairs, I noticed the telephone lying nearby, and I thought about picking it up and calling for help. I didn't think to call 911; instead, I thought of calling someone close, so I called my neighbor. A young child answered, and I pleaded, "Help me, please help me. Wake your aunt up. He has a baseball bat, and he's going to kill me. Please help." Then I heard him coming back up the stairs, so I quickly put the phone back exactly as it was. I thought that if he knew I had called someone, it would only make things worse. He continued to beat me. I screamed and screamed, crying out, "Oh my God, help me." He responded, "God's not going to help you tonight. This is me and Freddy Krueger's night." He named the bat Freddy Krueger.

The beating continued, and all I could remember is lying there with my hands and arms covering my head and face, screaming as loudly as I could. I thought I was going to die that night. His mission was to take my life. Someone once asked me why I didn't do this or that, and I replied, "Have you ever faced death in your life?" I was facing death. I can't even begin to explain the pain because you feel it, but you don't fully comprehend it. I just wondered when this beating would finally end. Survival instincts kicked in, and that meant not doing anything to make him angrier. At one point, after I cried out for God's help, he swung the bat again, but this time, I mustered some strength and grabbed hold of the bat, causing him to pull me up off the floor. We locked eyes, and I asked him, "Why? Why are you beating me like this? What about our children? If you kill me, they won't have a mother to raise them."

In that moment, it was as if he came to his senses. He threw me back on the bed and said, "Take me to get my children." He was yelling at me to put some clothes on because I was only wearing my bra and underwear. I reached for my jeans that were nearby and managed to put them on, all while he stood there watching. Then, I had to make it to the bathroom to clean myself up. I dragged myself along the walls, using them for support, as he observed me. Eventually, I made it out of the room and into the bathroom. I leaned against the sink and looked in the mirror, seeing the blood running down my face. He screamed at me, "Wash your face! Wash your face! You look a mess. You're not going behind me looking like that."

At that moment, I began to hear sirens, and he took off running. I can still picture myself standing there in that bloody bathroom, my whole life shattered. This man believed that if he couldn't have me, no one else could. The police burst through the front door, shouting, "Who is upstairs? Come down!" I called out to them, telling them that I was alone and unable to walk. They rushed upstairs with guns, ensuring that I was alone and coming to my rescue. They found a severely beaten ninety-eight-pound woman. I was quickly rushed to the emergency room at the hospital where I worked. I pleaded with them to call my cousin and my brother. Within seconds, my cousin was there. She said she was so scared because she didn't know where he was or what he was thinking, but she was there. I know it pained her to see me like that. We were raised together and were more like sisters than cousins.

Later, my uncle came, and I could see the hurt in their eyes as they watched me lie there. There was a girl who saw me, and I heard her say, "Oh my God, it looks like Mike Tyson got a hold of her." Many friends from work came to see me, and it was the worst feeling ever. I remember feeling incredibly thirsty but not being allowed to drink anything. I underwent x-ray after x-ray. Finally, they moved me to a room. I longed to see my children and kept asking for them. My cousin brought them up, but I didn't realize how bad I looked. If I had known, I might not have wanted them to come in. My kids entered the room, took one look at me, began screaming, and ran back out the door. I cried, wondering why. Later, I learned that my face was so swollen and that I was wrapped from head to foot, making it difficult to recognize me.

With that baseball bat, he delivered two blows to my head. My right elbow was busted, and pins had to be put in. My left arm and left ankle were broken, requiring bolts to be inserted. The main bone in my right leg was also broken. I had several cracked ribs and a punctured liver. I had lost so much blood that night, and they had to give me several pints to replenish it. The doctors told my family that it was a good thing I had so much alcohol in my body because it saved my life due to the amount of blood I had lost. They also informed my family that I might never walk again, and if by some miracle I did, I would have a limp. My girlfriend told me that my head looked like the size of a watermelon. The initial room they placed me in had to be changed because there were threats that he would come to the hospital and finish what he had started. So they moved me right next to the nurse's desk and provided them with a picture of him.

They also stationed a police officer to watch my room. A friend of mine did inform the police that they had seen him on the hospital grounds, but nothing ever came of it. It was a chaotic situation. I was a twenty-five-year-old woman who had once been able to care for herself and her kids, but now I couldn't. I can't even begin to explain how I felt.

My whole life is in ruins. I couldn't even think about helping my children, even if I wanted to, because I needed help myself. Helpless. I don't remember much from my first few nights at the hospital, probably because I was heavily medicated for the pain. I believe I had surgery the next day and was placed in four casts. My family took my kids and moved them to a different school out of fear that he might try to take them. He was still out and about, walking around with the baseball bat that had my blood on it, bragging about what he had done until some people were ready to confront him. My aunt and family from Pennsylvania immediately came down to attend to the situation. It was a blessing because even though we hadn't been in constant contact since I had left, they showed their love by dropping everything and traveling such a long distance to support me and my children. I received an outpouring of love from so many people. My coworkers at the hospital were there, caring for me. The people in the dietary department, where I worked, were especially supportive.

Every day, someone was there to check on me around the clock. Some would come to feed me and simply be there with me. Believe it or not, the guy who had left me had the audacity to come to the hospital, and my cousin from Pennsylvania grabbed him by the collar in the hallway and asked why he had left me like that. His response was that he got knocked out of the window and went to get help. On one occasion, my brothers were in the room with me when a man entered who knew the father of my children. As it turns out, he worked for the family. He later confessed that he had been sent there to see the extent of my injuries, but I think when he actually witnessed it, it was too much for him. I was truly severely beaten. They described me as a mummy. My legs were attached to a crane-like device to keep them elevated, and my arms were propped up. I do remember that I had to be turned slightly at times because it was so painful on my sides, and I later found out it was due to the cracked ribs. Another doctor came immediately to check on me because there was concern that the tumor had burst.

God is good because the tumor was found in the same spot where they had initially discovered it. Just think, he could have hit me with one blow, considering my cracked ribs were so close. Lord, I thank you because I could have died from that as well. The most painful day was when my children had to leave and go back to Pennsylvania with my family. It hurt so bad, but I believed it was for their own good. My children now tell me that they were taken back to the apartment to gather some things before leaving, and they describe how the house looked. They said there was blood everywhere—on the walls and floor, smeared from the room to the bathroom—and there were big holes in the walls where he tried to hit me but missed, hitting the walls instead.

I can't even imagine how they felt seeing all of that, knowing it was their home and their mother's blood, and the holes were a result of their father trying to beat their mother to death. Now they had to go to the hospital to say goodbye and move to another state with a family they didn't really know. And then the day came for them to leave. My legs were connected to some sort of crane-like device, I suppose to elevate them and prevent blood clots or something. This time when the kids came to say goodbye, my leg was down and my son accidentally bumped into it and pulled it. I screamed in pain. He started crying so hard, and I couldn't even hug him because of the casts. They said goodbye to me, and I told them how much I loved them. We cried and cried. I promised them that I would get well and be there with them. I felt like I had lost everything. My babies were leaving. Helpless was how I felt. They had to leave, and I had a long road to recovery. I am still in the birthing position that I talked about at the beginning of this chapter.

A few times, I had to go to rehab to learn how to walk with my casts. They had to create a special tool for me to eat with because I couldn't bend my elbows to feed myself. They said I had a crane-like contraption over me, with my legs and arms hooked up so they could be raised in the air. My coworkers were incredibly kind to me. They would come up to help feed me and, if not that, to uplift my spirits. Such a wonderful group of people. And it wasn't just them, so many other friends came to check on me. Despite the immense pain I was in, I made sure they made sure I looked nice. I even remember my cousin trying to apply a little makeup and lipstick. It may sound strange, but it's the truth. I can recall some of the staff in the emergency room saying that considering how bad my condition was, I seemed to be one of the most resilient patients they had ever seen. I was still spirited, to some extent. And even today, you'll find me to be that way. I suppose it's the God in me.

The day finally arrived for me to leave the hospital. I was now in a wheelchair. I went to live with my cousin and her family. I was so heartbroken. My children were miles away from me, and I could only talk to them on the telephone. My daughter's birthday was coming up at the end of the month, and it pained me deeply that I couldn't be there with her.

The hospital had collected some money for me, and a close girlfriend of mine took the money and bought things I needed. I asked her to get a card and put some cash in it to send to my daughter. It was the most I could do. When my son got on the phone, he would cry and cry, saying, "Mommy, I want you." It was excruciatingly painful. I felt utterly crushed. Not only did I feel hurt hearing my kids on the other end of the phone, but now I had to rely on my family to take care of me. My cousin would have to leave for work, and she had two daughters who became my nurses and angels. We had always been very close. They were fifteen and sixteen years old. These girls took exceptional care of me. They had to assist me with bedpans, wash me, dress me—they had to care for me like a baby. And they did just that. I can never forget these girls because they showered me with love. They often share stories of how their mom would come home, and I would get them in trouble by saying they hadn't done something, and their mom would reprimand them, while I would sit back and laugh. They say their mom was serious about ensuring I received the best care. They also recount how I was so afraid that my abuser would come back and get me.

There was one night when I thought I heard him trying to come up to the window to get in, and I was screaming while they were screaming and trying to get me up and move the bed for our safety. I was so skinny, around ninety pounds, and they would pick me up like a baby sometimes to move me from place to place. I had a big wound on the top of my head, and they had to cut my hair around that area to keep it clean. I also remember feeling very embarrassed in that condition. I only had two outfits to wear: a blue and burgundy sweat suit, the only things that provided comfort. I would sit out on the porch, and people would stare. I even remember seeing the wife of the man I had dated after my overdose and mental health stay. I wasn't the cause of their breakup, but she knew about me, and sometimes when people are separated in a marriage and there are children involved, the woman may feel upset because they think you're taking something away from their kids. I felt terrible.

Even though I had excellent caregivers, I was only twenty-five years old. I've always been the type that can't be kept down. One day they came home and found me up and walking in my four casts. I had taught myself how to get up out of that wheelchair and walk. I remember standing at the stove cooking an egg, and my brother walked in, shocked. From that time on, I was up and walking in my casts. But one day, on my way back from the doctor's, I saw the guy who had driven the trunk on the night of my attack. They had released him from jail. I lost it. I felt that if they let him out, they would let my children's father out too. By that time, he had been arrested. I remember thinking I had to leave my cousin's house because if he got out, he would come there to find me. I called up one of my best friends and told her I was coming to stay with her. They took me to her house. This is when I started drinking heavily in my condition. I would play Al Green and drink until I was drunk. I wanted to numb the pain.

They found me one time on the bathroom floor, drunk, crying, and trying to pull my casts off. I was an emotional wreck. Life was becoming overwhelming. I could hear the cries of my children on the phone, and I was in four casts, afraid that they would release the man who had hurt me. This went on for a while. I resorted to drinking and even began smoking crack, anything to numb the pain. My family had moved all of my belongings out of my apartment, and they sold whatever they could to provide me with money to get to Pennsylvania. I took every bit of that money and spent it on drinking. There were times when I would even go to a crack house with someone, still wearing my casts, and get high. I know it wasn't right, but I was hurting.

My girlfriend and her husband did everything they could to make me happy. However, there was one day when we didn't have any money and her husband was at work. I was crying and upset, craving a drink. She scrounged up all the change she could find in the house just to get me some beer. The day finally came for me to go to the doctor to have my casts removed. The doctors were amazed that I walked into their office in my casts, but when they removed them, I began walking as if nothing had happened. I remember the doctors telling me that I was a walking miracle. That same night, I drove a car, even though I was mentally messed up. I got together with a friend and drove their car. We went to smoke some crack. I was now free from the casts, but mentally I was still struggling. I needed to leave North Carolina and go see about my children.

There was an older guy who had always been crazy about me and would do anything for me. And he did just that. He bought my ticket to Pennsylvania and also gave me spending money, but I ended up drinking and smoking crack. I used up all the money. You are probably thinking, *Well, she didn't care too much about going to be with her children if she used up all the funds the way that she did.* But I did care more than you can imagine even though I was mentally and emotionally damaged. That was my coping method to calm my pain. It's easy to say till you walk in my shoes.

I sweet-talked the older guy once again to buy me a one-way ticket to Pennsylvania. He did, but this time he took me himself, bought the ticket, and I got on the bus traveling to Pennsylvania.

I'm still in the birthing position, waiting for a new beginning.

CHAPTER 8

Bag Lady

Come unto me, all ye that labor and are
heavy laden and I will give you rest.
—Matthew 11:28

As women, it is crucial for us to learn how to let go of our emotional baggage and address our issues before entering into new relationships. Why do we feel the need to jump from one relationship to another? Based on my own past experiences, I have come to the realization that despite always having people around me, I felt an underlying sense of loneliness. It was a loneliness that only God could fill, even though I was unaware of it at the time. I attempted to fill that void with alcohol, drugs, and men, but my spirit resembled that of a broken "bag lady" on the inside. I was truly broken.

The year after I arrived in Pennsylvania, I met someone. My son started exhibiting strange behavior, associating the man around me with what his father had done to me (even my baby carried baggage and had issues that affected him). During this time, I had a baby named Candace, whom I considered my angel. I entered into that relationship carrying all of my unresolved issues. I was twenty-five years old, and he was twenty-three. He walked away when I told him I was pregnant. I was still grappling with self-esteem issues. Let's talk about the three surgeries and the immense pain I experienced, all while wearing a mask to hide my true emotions.

On December 5, 1989, I boarded a Greyhound bus from Fayetteville to Pittsburgh, Pennsylvania. I had nothing but a red apple and the clothes on my back. I remember calling the kids to let them know I was coming, and that I was still in a wheelchair and would need their help. They sounded incredibly excited that mommy was coming to be with them. That night, I arrived at my cousin's house where the kids were living, and they were already fast asleep. I can still envision the joy in their eyes as they looked up and saw me standing over them. It was the most incredible feeling in the world. They jumped up, screaming and crying, "Mommy, Mommy!" Then they noticed I was walking, and their excitement grew even more. We hugged and cried tears of joy. I crawled into bed between them and slept soundly until the next morning.

Moving here was a little rough. I was already a mess, and I guess you could say I had a bit of a ghetto attitude. My cousin, on the other hand, was completely different. We were like night and day. I smoked cigarettes, drank, and partied, while she was more conservative. So we clashed. I remember when my kids came home from school, they seemed so different. One day, I asked myself, "Who are these kids?" They had become more conservative. I knew I had to find my own place soon. During my first weekend here, I met up with my godmother who lives in this area, and the kids and I stayed with her. We decided to go out, and we ended up at a bar. As we were sitting there, my eyes landed on a tall, dark, and handsome young guy wearing a nice brim hat. I thought, *Wow, who is this?* He turned around, looked in our direction, and smiled. Then I realized he was a friend from when I lived here before. Back then, he was just a young boy, but now he had grown into a handsome man. He sat with us, and we all talked and reminisced about the past when I lived here.

I have always wanted to do a seminar called "Bag Lady" because some of us do become that bag lady. She is a woman who doesn't take the time to clean up the mess from a previous relationship before jumping into another one. That was me. I had just come out of an abusive relationship, not fully healed physically or mentally, carrying a bag full of issues, and ready to start dating someone else. From that night, we exchanged numbers and started dating. I now had a boyfriend but was still living with my cousin. It wasn't working out. I had to get myself and my kids out of that house. I remember coming home one night, and she was fussing because I smelled like cigarette smoke and all sorts of things. I leaned against the wall, looking at her, and in my mind, I felt the urge to grab a butcher knife and harm her. It was definitely time to move.

The housing authority finally called and said there was an apartment available. The apartment had recently been in a fire, and you could still smell the smoke, but I didn't care, and I'm sure she didn't either. I just wanted my own place, and I knew she was ready for me to have it. We moved in, and on the first day, my kids and I had a big party. I let them go crazy, and we had fun. We were in our own place that we could now call home.

It was hard at first; I didn't know anyone, and the neighborhood was on a hill that I considered a mountain. The kids struggled to adjust and make new friends. They now tell me that starting over here was tough for them. One of the challenges was that they weren't used to living around white people. Coming from the South, we had never lived next door to a white person, let alone attended school with them. My daughter recalls how she had to be shown around the school by a white girl, and she didn't like it at all simply because she wasn't accustomed to it. Both of them spoke with a strong country accent, and no one could understand what they were saying, which made them targets for bullying. My son said he just stopped talking altogether. It's important for us to be mindful of how our children feel because I never thought about their emotions or considered that they were going through something like this. We often assume that since they are kids, they don't experience such deep feelings, but believe me, they do. The new man in my life started spending more and more time with us, and the kids adored him because he loved children and always played with them.

Despite their feelings, I now believe that they had thoughts in their minds about everything that had happened. One night we were getting ready to go out, and my son became upset. He was a mama's boy and would always stick close to me, but that night he was so angry about me going out that he said I should take a baseball bat and beat me like his dad did. I was devastated, and we all were to hear him say that. I remember giving him a spanking for saying such a thing, not realizing then how much he was hurting. It's important to remember that just because they smile on the outside doesn't mean they aren't crying on the inside. Also, we had never talked about what had happened. They only knew that their whole life had changed, we would never go back to North Carolina, and their dad was in jail. I continued my relationship with my boyfriend, and by now, he had moved in with us.

My house was the place where everyone gathered. A girlfriend of mine, along with her boyfriend and kids, would come over, as well as some other friends, and we would party. She used to tell people that you haven't truly experienced drinking and partying until you've done it with Vanessa. A few months later, I found out I was pregnant. Wow, just three months after everything I had been through, I was now expecting a baby. My boyfriend was scared of becoming a father and overwhelmed by the fact that I was pregnant, so he left me for a few weeks. He was afraid, and I was also afraid of bringing a new life into the world when I wasn't mentally prepared. I often wondered what my kids were thinking during this time. As I grew bigger, my son would crawl up on my stomach and lay there all the time. I really didn't have much, but I had a girlfriend who stuck by me and provided so much support. She became my daughter's godmother. Despite my fears, as I mentioned in a previous chapter, bringing a new life into this world requires strength, and after hearing my baby's heartbeat, my thoughts changed. This was my baby, and I felt excited. The same went for her dad; I knew he would be okay because he loved children, he just needed some time to digest the idea of becoming a father.

Then on December 5, 1990, exactly one year after I arrived in Pennsylvania, I gave birth to a beautiful little girl named Candis. I couldn't decide on a name, and my daughter's godmother and I tried and tried to come up with one. One day, while watching Full House, at the end of the show they would display the character's real name. One character's real name was Candace, and I thought, "Oh wow, that's different," and I instantly fell in love with the name. So when my daughter was born, we named her *Candis*, spelled differently but pronounced the same. I love the name *Candis*. I call her my angel, and I truly mean it because carrying her, I knew I had to try and get myself together. Not that I didn't do it for my other kids, but I didn't want to do anything that could harm her birth, such as bringing her into the world with drugs and alcohol. Her dad was there, and despite his initial fears, he became a proud father from that moment on.

When I became pregnant, I remember informing the doctors about my tumor, and some of them seemed to dismiss it, as if they had never encountered such a case before.

They referred me to a few doctors to find someone who could remove it. Eventually, I found a doctor who understood my situation and assured me that he would remove the tumor after I gave birth. Additionally, I needed to have the pins and bolts removed from my previous injury. So I ended up having three surgeries done at once: the removal of the tumor, the extraction of pins and bolts, and getting my tubes tied. The medical staff placed me on the maternity floor, treating me for the removal of my tubes and tumor, unaware of the bolts and pins in my ankle and elbow. It brought back painful memories of being in casts again; it was a terrible experience. They instructed me to walk to some extent, but I kept insisting that I couldn't put too much pressure on my ankle. Unfortunately, one of the nurses, possibly overlooking the details in my reports, had me stand, and it caused me to scream in agony. The pain was excruciating. Eventually, I was discharged to go home and take care of my baby and other children. They provided me with a walking cane, perhaps because removing the bolts from my ankle might have left it weaker at times. However, I stowed away the cane in a closet and never used it. I do remember accidentally bumping my elbow and causing it to bleed, but apart from that, I was fine.

CHAPTER 9

The Spirit of the Lord Was Upon Me

The Spirit of the Lord is upon me, because he hath
anointed me to preach the gospel to the poor; he
hath sent me to heal the brokenhearted, to preach
deliverance to the captives, and recovering of sight to
the blind, to set at liberty them that are bruised.

—Luke 4:18

I can still remember how my brother would constantly pester me to accompany him to church. He would plead with me repeatedly, and one Sunday, I finally gave in. The irony was that I had been under the influence of drugs the night before, yet there I was, finding myself at the altar, surrendering my life to the Lord in response to the preacher's call and my brother's persistent nudging. Little did I know at that moment, this seemingly trivial decision would mark the beginning of a profoundly transformative journey. It reignited a spark within me, one that I had long forgotten existed, a dormant flame that would take me two decades to recollect.

In this chapter I talk about the following:

- Revisiting your past
- The question that you had in your mind of the woman that prayed for you on your death bed
- Her asking you to accept the Lord
- Not being able to say the words but mumbling
- How you believe that you accepted Him right then
- How people who saw you and saw what you came through know that they witnessed a miracle

After giving birth to my daughter, I tried to navigate through life, attempting to fulfill the roles of a mother, girlfriend, and friend. However, deep down, I was slowly withering away. I found myself returning to the party scene, indulging in reckless behavior. Friends would come over, and we would get the children settled before diving into our revelry. One of my girlfriends even remarked that they loved coming to my house because "you haven't truly experienced drinking until you've done it with Vanessa." We would savor those alcohol-soaked cherries, accompanied by my beloved Budweiser and gin, not to mention the Newport 100 cigarettes. Little did they know, I was tormented on the inside, concealing my pain from everyone, including my boyfriend. After they left at night, and the children were asleep, I would find myself weeping uncontrollably. I despised living in Pennsylvania, consumed by anger. I held an intense hatred towards my children's father for the agony he had inflicted upon us. Even when I was in my wheelchair, fresh out of the hospital, I remember contemplating going to the jail and seeking vengeance on him. And even after regaining my ability to walk, those feelings persisted. He had shattered our lives.

As my drinking spiraled further out of control, there were times when I would sit alone, drowning a whole case of beer while tears streamed down my face. I was wearing a mask, portraying a facade of normalcy in front of others, but once everyone departed and I was left alone, the mask would come off, and I would weep inconsolably. Slowly but surely, I fell back into using crack cocaine, all the while concealing it meticulously. Once again, the mask became my shield. My boyfriend remained oblivious to my struggles, perhaps perceiving me as unstable due to my erratic behavior, but I couldn't let him or my friends who I spent time with know about my secret. This was my coping mechanism, my way of numbing the excruciating pain I was enduring. Meanwhile, the father of my children was sentenced to prison. I watched a television show where a man, recently released from prison, hunted down his victim with a hammer. The woman had never been notified of his release. This terrified me. I was gripped by the fear that a similar fate awaited me. So, I made it my mission to find out which prison he was in and began corresponding with him. It wasn't that I wanted him back, but I needed to know every detail of his whereabouts. He would draw pictures of the children and send letters regularly. As long as I had the prison address, I felt a false sense of security, but it did nothing to alleviate the profound pain I carried within.

My brother came to stay with me and witnessed the extent of my drinking problem. He had his own struggles, having been in and out of trouble for most of his life, but he always turned to church. I had never been to church and had no interest in it. However, he persistently pleaded with me to accompany him one Sunday morning. Reluctantly, I agreed, even though I had a terrible hangover. I paid no attention to the preaching or the singing. Then came the altar call, and my brother urged me to go up. I resisted, arguing with him right there in the church. I finally relented, thinking that if it made him happy, I would go. I went up and surrendered my life to Christ. When I returned home, I tried to do whatever I thought was necessary to be saved. I stopped drinking and made an effort to do what was right. I made two requests to the Lord—I asked for a car and a job. I promised that if I received those things, I would attend church faithfully and tithe. Miraculously, God granted my requests. I was hired at the hospital, and I obtained my first little car.

Life started to improve. But as they say, the devil comes to distract. And that's exactly what happened. Another one of my brothers came to live with me. This was the same brother I used to party with back in the South, and now he was here with me. Naturally, the drinking began again. I had turned my back on God and the promise I made to Him. Now I had all three of my brothers coming and going from my house, and the partying resumed. Drugs re-entered the picture as well. I made sure my children were taken care of and the bills were paid, and there was food in the house, but after that, it was party time. The car I had asked God for never made it to church; it could be found at every bar in town. I also failed to tithe from the paycheck I received from the hospital. I always say, "Don't play with God," because He stripped me of everything He had given me. My drinking had become so severe that I started missing work. On my birthday weekend, I had to work. I remember some friends saying, "Come on, let's party." I replied, "No, I have to get up for work." They insisted that a few drinks wouldn't hurt. Little did I know, it would hurt. I went out that night, and the next morning, I was supposed to be at work at six o'clock.

A friend from work called and said, "Vanessa, where are you? You're supposed to be at work." I was too hungover to even go. On Monday, I went to work and completed my entire shift. At the end, I was called into the office and informed that I had been fired. I lost the job God had given me, and the car my boyfriend and I were driving broke down on the highway. We managed to get the car running again, and I found a job at the mental health building where I had to be at work by five thirty in the morning to prepare breakfast for the patients. There were days when my brother and I had stayed up all night drinking and getting high, and I hadn't even slept before going to work. I laugh now because I remember being so high and messed up that the patients looked at me like I should be on the other side of the table with them. Things were really deteriorating. Although we got the car up and running, my boyfriend was trying to work amidst all the chaos. All of us had access to the car. One Friday, he got paid and filled the gas tank to ensure he could commute to work.

One night, my brother took the car and drove it until the tank was empty. My boyfriend was furious. He confronted my brother, and it escalated into a big fight. They were breaking lamps and tables—it was a terrible scene. Someone called the police. In panic, I set my baby down and went into the kitchen to grab a butcher knife. I believe I blanked out because I was so afraid that my boyfriend was going to seriously harm my brother, who had just been diagnosed with a serious heart condition. As I was returning from the kitchen with the knife, the police entered the house. One of the officers drew his gun and told me to drop the knife. I complied with his command. I picked up my baby and went out the back door to take her to the neighbor's house. When I returned to the apartment, the cop was arresting my brother and boyfriend. He then said, "Arrest her too." Another officer asked, "Arrest her for what?" The cop replied, "Because she was coming at me with a butcher knife." I was handcuffed, and the three of us were taken to the police station, where we all spent the night in jail. The cop told me I was lucky because he had considered using his .357 gun on me.

I later discovered that this particular cop had been severely beaten by some young black boys a few months prior to my incident, so every time he encountered black individuals, he panicked, recalling how he had been attacked. They said I was fortunate that he didn't shoot me. I was charged with attempted murder of a police officer and assault with a deadly weapon. Oh my God. Devastation struck once again. I was terrified at the thought of potentially facing jail time. I had three children. On the day of my court appearance, we all believed that the cop wouldn't show up, but he did. However, it ultimately worked in my favor, though I didn't realize it then. Now, I give all the glory to God. I ended up with ARD probation, community service, and a fine exceeding $1,000.

After this incident, my brother sought help and went to rehab. My boyfriend and I had separated but remained friends, and he always had custody of his daughter. I continued working at the mental health building, and I remember one day at work, as it neared the end of my shift, an inexplicable feeling washed over me. Remember, I was still in the birthing position. I began to cry, tears streaming down my face.

When I was in the hospital, I remember a woman kneeling at my bedside, praying. I didn't recall who she was. For over twenty years, I questioned who had prayed for me in my hospital room. We found some old friends on Facebook, and I called one of them. She was my neighbor. She said, "Vanessa, do you remember me coming to see you and my aunt praying for you?" I replied, "No." She proceeded to tell me that she had visited me and when she saw me, her heart dropped. She didn't think I would make it. She described how I was bandaged up like a mummy and how swollen I was. She ran to get her aunt, who was a preacher, and pleaded with them, "Please, please come pray for my friend. I don't think she is going to make it." They agreed, and despite my friend not living for the Lord at the time, she had faith that the prayer would bring about change.

When they arrived at the hospital, they entered my room, and her aunt fell at my bedside and began to pray, while all I could do was mumble. When her aunt finished, she said, "The Lord said this child will walk again." My friend recounted how the room suddenly became very bright. I believe it was on that day that I gave my life to Christ. The Lord's hand had been upon me all the way back then, and even when I hit rock bottom again, His hand was extended wide, inviting me to come and find rest. He had a plan for my life. On that day, I didn't immediately turn my life around, but the process had begun.

When Distraction Comes

*And this I speak for your own profit; not that I may cast
a snare upon you, but for that which is comely, and that
ye may attend upon the Lord without distraction.*
—1 Corinthians 7:35

At this stage of my life, I was striving to do the right thing, but it was a challenge for me. We often hear the phrase "The devil made me do it," but as believers, we need to recognize that it's not the devil who is responsible, but rather the many distractions and lack of self-control in our lives.

My older brother came to visit, and the party started all over again. This sent me into a tailspin, and I found myself once again caught up in distractions and not living a saved life. I began bargaining with God for a job, a car, and other things, but I failed to follow through on the promises I made to Him. Living with three brothers and my boyfriend, the situation became chaotic. The car had no gas, and tensions escalated, resulting in a fight between my boyfriend and one of my brothers. Seeing my brother in danger, I instinctively came to his rescue, but I blacked out for a moment. When I regained awareness, I found myself holding a knife with a police officer standing before me, gun drawn. It felt as if I was facing death once again, as the cop threatened to shoot me. The events that followed led to my incarceration, and in court, I relied on God as my lawyer. Eventually, I found a job at a mental health facility, but I went to work hungover, realizing that I should have been a patient there instead.

CHAPTER 11

Drawing of the Holy Spirit

*In whom ye also trusted, after that ye heard the word of
truth, the gospel of your salvation: in whom also after that ye
believed, ye were sealed with that Holy Spirit of promise.*
—Ephesians 1:13

I remember the day I went to pick up Candace, and I felt
something stirring inside me, though at the time I couldn't
quite comprehend it. Looking back now, I know it was the
Holy Spirit drawing me closer. I took the jitney to get my
baby, but I couldn't stop crying. I wept and wept, feeling a
deep need for someone from the church to come and pray
with me. As time went on, my life began to change, and a
different kind of man entered the picture. My cousin introduced me to my husband. We met at a bar, and despite being
saved, I still went out occasionally, seeking deliverance from
the demons that had held me captive for so long. I continued
to wear my mask, hiding the struggles beneath.

In our first conversation that night, it felt as if no one else
existed in the room. We talked for months over the phone,
and he treated me with the utmost respect and kindness. No
one had ever treated me that way before. I became scared and

distanced myself from him, convinced that I didn't deserve such a man. He introduced me to his mom at the Family Dollar store. He had his life together, and the enemy whispered in my ear, telling me I wasn't worthy of this man.

Things weren't going well between me and my daughter's father. We were two different people, around the same age but carrying different burdens. Today, he is still a great man and a wonderful father. Perhaps we could have stayed together, but I had too much going on in my life, things he was never aware of. I remember trying to tell him many times, but the words never came out. Then, one day, we took the kids out to the park, and I apologized to him, expressing my regrets if I had caused him any pain. Our relationship had its share of ups and downs, but I was grateful for the beautiful daughter we shared. Ladies, let's remember to address our baggage before jumping into a new relationship.

One night, feeling down about not finding the right man, I went out with my godmother. I was lamenting about the lack of good men and feeling discouraged. She suggested we go to the club and listen to some oldies music, which I loved. As we entered the club, I noticed a friend of mine at the bar, and while ordering a drink, I shared my woes with her. The guy sitting next to her overheard and boldly claimed, "I'm a good man." I looked at him skeptically, thinking, "Yeah, right." But deep down, I couldn't help but notice his attractive features—lovely brown eyes and nice hair. I returned to my seat, and we exchanged glances. Eventually, he mustered the courage to approach my table, and little did I know that this encounter marked the beginning of a new life for me. We talked and talked, losing ourselves in conversation as if no one else existed in the room. He opened up about his past experiences, and I shared my own journey.

When the night came to an end, he asked for my phone number, but I hesitated, telling him that I don't usually give out my number. Instead, I suggested he get in touch with his cousin, who was my friend. There was something different about him that intrigued me, and I wanted to learn more. As I asked around, everyone had nothing but good things to say about him. A few weeks went by, and I can't quite recall the details, but my baby's father and I attempted to reconcile once again. However, it didn't work out, and we ended up in a minor argument. During the altercation, he pushed me, and I got hit in the mouth, resulting in the need for a couple of stitches at the hospital.

At the hospital, while tearfully expressing my frustration to the nurse about not finding a good man and thinking I would never meet Mr. Right, she reassured me, saying, "Don't worry, honey, you will find a good man." Little did I know, the guy I had met at the bar would eventually reach out to me. It happened about a month later. We started talking on the phone, and soon, we were conversing every day. We spent a month building a connection over the phone before deciding to meet face to face. Meanwhile, I had also returned to church during this time, marking the continuation of my transformation. I joined the choir, and life began to improve. Something profound had taken hold of me, and I knew it was the Lord. He had decided to take me out to dinner, and I felt nervous because there was something special about this man. He managed to captivate my attention through our daily phone conversations. I remember the evening of our planned outing, and I was quite anxious because I didn't have any nice clothes for the occasion. My babysitter provided me with an outfit to wear that evening. This man was unlike anyone I had ever dated before. He was a true gentleman. After he dropped me off at home, the night came to an end, but we continued to talk. I was drawn to him.

One day, while at the Family Dollar store, I was about to purchase a pair of earrings, and to my surprise, he and his mother appeared. I clutched the earrings tightly in my hand, feeling embarrassed to let him see me buying jewelry from this store. He introduced me to his mother and declared, "This is going to be my new lady." From that day on, I arranged for my baby to stay with her father for a few days, while I took my other children to stay with my sister-in-law for a short period.

A few days passed during which I stayed in a drunken state. Why? Because my self-esteem was so low that I believed there had to be something wrong with this man liking me. I mean, I was barely ninety pounds. I was a woman who had struggled with crack addiction and was on the brink of alcoholism. I genuinely believed I wasn't good enough for him. Thankfully, my sister-in-law talked some sense into me, and I went home and called him. As women, we can be so burdened by life's circumstances that when something good comes our way, we tend to run from it. Regardless of what we've been through or what men may say about us or call us, we have to know our true worth and refuse to let someone dictate who we can be or become. We need to stand tall. And that's where I was at that time.

We started talking and seeing each other more, and I continued attending church, where I drew my strength. Before I knew it, I had quit drinking and smoking crack. I simply stopped. Life was beginning to take on a different per-spective. My love for Christ and for him grew stronger and stronger. Eventually, I introduced him to the children, and their joy was overwhelming. One day, he said, "We're going to change your whole apartment." This man came in and painted my entire downstairs, refurnished the entire apart-ment. He would take me to the store and encourage me to try on outfit after outfit. Then we would go home with four or five new outfits, matching shoes, jewelry, and more. I felt like Cinderella. The kids were being spoiled left and right.

While all of this was happening in the physical realm, in the spiritual realm, I was also being blessed. I used to curse a lot, but one day, God cleaned up my mouth. He delivered me from drugs, alcohol, and even cursing. Oh, my God! I was truly falling more in love with God, and this time when I rededicated my life, I knew it was for real. Friends changed, places changed, and I was changing. God was truly revealing Himself to me.

Additionally, regarding the $1,000 fine I had received from the charge involving the police officer, my boyfriend and I went to the courthouse. I had to check in with my sponsor every so often, and it's true what they say: God becomes our lawyer in the courtroom. The judge informed us that my fine had been wiped clean. I don't know what happened, all I know is that God is good. However, despite all the blessings happening for me and to me, there was still a part of me that was hurting. I was angry and still harbored hatred toward my children's father. You see, we can claim to be saved and say we're living for God, as I was, but still carry a heart full of hate. God wanted to do more in us and through us, but we hold on to things from our past.

When this happened, I felt stuck. Then one night, God said, "You have to forgive your children's father." I thought, "No way God is talking to me. How can I forgive a man who has beaten me and ruined my life and my children's lives?" But God persisted, pricking my heart. It didn't happen right away, but He continued to work on me. It had been a while since I had been home, and both the kids and I longed to visit our old home. This would be the first time since 1989. So my boyfriend said, "If you all want to go home, then plan the trip." We decided to go in July 1993. We were beyond excited. My brother was joining us too. However, the day before we left, I received a call from my children's aunt with devastating news. She said, "I have bad news for you. The kids' grandmother has passed away." She had been sick for a while, and she knew we were coming down to visit. She had always loved my kids dearly and wanted to see them. She tried to hold on, but the Lord took her the day before our visit. So now, not only were we going to visit home, but we were also going to a funeral—my children's grandmother's funeral. We made it to the South, and the sight of the sign that said "Fayetteville, North Carolina" filled us with joy. Truly, there's no place like home. People were shocked to see how much the kids had grown. I remember visiting the hospital where I had once worked, and it felt strange because hardly anyone recognized me. I had gained weight and looked like a different person. I tried to be there for my boyfriend, as it was his first time visiting my hometown, but with the passing of their grandmother, there were two things happening simultaneously. I had to be there for my kids as well. I had never turned my kids against their dad. I never badmouthed him or spoke ill of him. I always believed that it was up to them to form their own opinions and feelings about him as they grew older. Even today, they don't hate their dad, but they don't like what he did. So when we arrived in the South, they wanted to see their dad. His sister had plans to take them to the prison to visit him. Since it was the first time seeing him since the incident, I wanted to be there with them. So when she took them, I went along too. It was my first time seeing him since the beating.

I remember when we arrived, we all sat together, and he mostly spoke to the kids. He was excited about how much they had grown and shared that his mother had passed away. That dominated most of the conversation. However, there was a moment of silence, and during that moment, I couldn't help but stare at his hand, remembering that it was the same hand that had wielded a baseball bat against my body. He then looked at me and said, "Vanessa, Vanessa, Vanessa." I immediately got up and moved. I knew he was looking at me in a way that I never wanted to see again. Then the day of the funeral arrived. People were everywhere. As we got there, the first person I saw was their dad. He stood there with two guards, handcuffed and shackled. The kids saw him and went straight to him. We stood there with him until it was time to go inside. Walking into a funeral side by side with the man who had tried to take my life made me believe in God. As we walked in, two by two, the kids in front and him and me behind them, I wondered what people thought.

After we sat down and the funeral began, I found myself staring at his hand and reflecting on that night when he attacked me with a baseball bat, trying to end my life. I had to shake him a few times because he was nodding off to sleep. Tears were rolling down the faces of various people, grieving their own losses. I shed tears as well, but some of my tears were tears of joy. I thanked God for how far He had brought me and for saving me, not allowing the enemy to take my life. It was at that moment that I truly believe I was able to forgive him, as the Lord had asked me to. My eyes were truly opened.

As I looked at him and reflected on my life, I realized how blessed I am. I should have been dead, but I am alive. I should have needed a wheelchair or a cane to walk into that funeral, but I walked in on my own. I shouldn't have looked any better than a drug addict or an alcoholic, but God had cleaned me up so much that people didn't even recognize me. Even when the Lord cleaned up my foul mouth, someone noticed because they said, "You even talk differently." So being able to sit beside someone who had beaten me with a baseball bat and still be in my right mind, I could do nothing else but obey the Lord's command to forgive.

See, I had been in handcuffs and shackles, not in the physical sense, but spiritually. The day I surrendered to God and forgave him from my heart, all my shackles and cuffs broke free. He was shackled and cuffed by the system, and when he served his required time, he was set free. I, on the other hand, was shackled and cuffed by the devil, bound by hate, unforgiveness, bitterness, and more, preventing me from becoming the woman God had called me to be. The moment I surrendered, I was released and set free to live, love, and be the woman He intended me to be. People, forgiveness is immensely important. God requires it from us, and it is the key to our future. We must not hold onto the pains and hurts of the past. Whether it was abuse, rape, being motherless or fatherless, we must understand that these are the roads of life we have to navigate. God has mapped out our lives since birth; He knows the end. He has things He wants us to do, but there are also things He tells us to do. If we simply fulfill the requirements, such as forgiveness, life can be remarkably different. There is immense power in forgiveness.

Now the birthing I kept speaking about occurred in the deliverance room at the funeral. I gave birth that day to what God wanted me to do, and that was forgiveness. I was completely free in my spirit, able to tell others that they can be free too. I also pray that God will save him as well. The funeral came to an end, and when it was time to leave, it was heartbreaking for my children because they had to leave their dad. My daughter took it particularly hard, screaming and crying, pleading not to take her daddy. She ran back to grab him, while my son held close to me, tears streaming down his face. My heart truly broke for them because I knew they loved and still love their dad. The trip was over, and we were on our way back to Pennsylvania. During this trip, I had removed my mask, and God did some deep healing within me. We arrived back home, and my love for God grew even deeper. My boyfriend and I also grew closer, and the day came when he asked me to be his wife.

My goodness, yes! He was like a knight in shining armor. This man has been nothing but a gentleman to me, the kind of guy I never thought I would see myself with. He was twelve years older, but he was a clean-cut man. Most of my life, I had been with older men, but they were street guys, hardcore men. But above all, I knew this man loved me. He made me feel like somebody.

CHAPTER 12

New Life

The thief cometh not, but for to steal, and to kill,
and to destroy: I am come that they might have life,
and that they might have it more abundantly.
—John 10:10

This marked a significant shift in my life, as things were finally taking a positive turn. I had a brand-new apartment, fully furnished by my soon-to-be husband. It dawned on me that in order to fully embrace the blessings God had in store for me, I needed to let go of more than just my addictions; I needed to shed the weight of certain people as well. At this point, my husband-to-be had proposed, and I recognized the importance of leaving the past behind. I made the decision to ask my brother to leave. It was time for Vanessa to relinquish the role of a bag lady, carrying unnecessary burdens that held me down. I had successfully quit drinking and using drugs.

In this chapter, I will discuss the following topics:

- My experience as a functional addict in the past
- How I made the decision to give up addiction and found deliverance, experiencing true freedom
- My journey of growing closer to Christ, deepening my faith
- Reminiscing about my preference for Newport 100 cigarettes in the past
- The enemy's attempts to use cigarettes against me even after finding freedom
- A significant encounter with Sis Charlotte, who asked if I was tired of smoking and prayed over me during a prayer meeting at her house, leading to instant deliverance and a sense of freedom
- A particular incident where I was home alone and experienced a strong craving for a cigarette, but instead, I went and tore the entire pack to shreds, signaling a significant change to my children
- The decision to give up secular music and its impact on my spiritual journey
- The dreams I started having and the significance of a particular dream where my spirit came out of my body
- Emphasizing the importance of walking in total forgiveness, especially in relation to my ex
- Reflecting on the funeral of my ex's mother and the emotions it evoked
- The overwhelming passion and zeal I developed for the Lord

Well, I'm in the process of planning my wedding, and we just found another apartment to start our new life together. The children are thrilled, and everything is falling into place.

It's remarkable how God orchestrates the things He desires for your life. I have lived in various places, but never in an area where it seemed like everyone was a Christian. To top it off, my neighbor happened to be a preacher. It's incredible how God sets you up for the things He wants in your life. While I had already been saved in church, I had the privilege of meeting this lady preacher who deepened my understanding of the Word of God like never before. There is undeniable power in His word, and it drew me closer and closer to Jesus. The preacher would host prayer meetings at her house, and one night I attended. Although I had quit drinking, cursing, and smoking crack, I was still holding onto something God wanted me to be free from: my cigarettes. During the prayer meeting, this blind elderly lady approached me and asked if I wanted to be free from the bondage of smoking. Without hesitation, I said yes. After all, I hadn't seen Jesus smoking, and I didn't want to either. I desired to be just like Him.

These women began to pray over me, one placing her hand on my head and the other on my stomach, fervently praying and cursing that desire at its root. I felt the undeniable power of God that night. When I returned home, I knew deep within me that I was truly done with smoking. A profound change had occurred within me. Around that time, I was attending a nine-month course at school. The next morning, I woke up with no desire for a cigarette. During break time at school, I confidently announced to everyone that I no longer smoked because I had been delivered at a prayer meeting. I was filled with excitement. Some tried blowing smoke in my face, but I didn't care because I knew I had been set free. However, later that day, while I was home alone, the craving for a cigarette suddenly came over me. I immediately called a woman of God whom I knew and shared what I was experiencing. She encouraged me to pray, assuring me that God had this under control. As I hung up the phone, the Holy Spirit guided me downstairs, and on top of the refrigerator, there sat a brand-new pack of Newport cigarettes. The devil knew this and was attempting to test me. I took the pack of cigarettes and ripped them to pieces.

The children came home and were taken aback, thinking I had gone crazy because they knew how much I loved my cigarettes. What they were beginning to witness was the reality of Jesus in their mom's life. God truly revealed Himself to me that day. Then a day arrived when my spirit longed for something more. The children were playing outside, and my fiancé had music playing. I kept searching for the right song, playing tracks by the O'Jays and the Whispers, but none of them felt right. Finally, I stumbled upon a CD by Hezekiah Walker and The Love Fellowship Crusade Choir. There was a song that said, "I hear You calling my name," and it resonated deeply within my spirit. Tears streamed down my face, and I went next door to see my neighbor. She told me, "Vanessa, God is truly pulling at your heart. He has great things in store for you; there is a ministry He has prepared for you." That day marked a true transformation in my life. I also realized that I needed to forgive the man who fathered my two children, despite the fact that he had beaten me nearly to death. But I did it. I forgave him and began to pray for him.

Even after I got married, there were times when I would have flashbacks of the things I had been through. I vividly recall a particular incident when one of the children accidentally spilled soda on the floor, and my husband asked, "Who did this? Who spilled this soda?" Without thinking, I immediately responded, "Oh my God, I will clean it up." I grabbed some paper towels, dropped to my knees, and started wiping the floor. As I cleaned, I looked up and saw my husband standing there, wearing a puzzled expression. In that moment, I burst into tears because I recognized familiar patterns from my abusive past that were trying to cling to me. Those baggage I mentioned earlier, ladies, that was one of mine. I cried out to God, praying for His help, declaring that I didn't want to be like that anymore. Every time I noticed old patterns resurfacing, even as I was on fire for the Lord, I would pray, "Lord, cleanse me of this garbage in my bag." There were things He needed to purify within me in order for me to fulfill the work He had called me to do.

When my son was just three months old, his father attacked me one night. After the fight, we went to bed. Our son was peacefully sleeping between us. As I lay there crying, I pleaded with God, saying, "Please help me. Get me out of this situation. I'm tired of being beaten." Suddenly, my eyes closed completely, and my spirit departed from my body. I watched from above as my spirit floated upward, observing my son, his father, and myself lying there. My spirit continued ascending, entering a narrow tunnel that gradually widened. People were gathered on either side, whispering and murmuring as I reached the end of the tunnel, where a brilliant light awaited me. Someone spoke to me, but I never knew the words. In an instant, I moved backward at an incredible speed, and my spirit reentered my body. I opened my eyes and jolted awake, frightened and bewildered by what had just occurred.

After getting saved, I discovered that there was a ministry waiting for me. An out-of-body experience revealed to me that the Lord had work for me to do here on earth. I realized then that all the suffering I had endured was for the glory of God. I was truly on fire for God, and He started giving me dreams that would later come true. My fiancé and I faced some obstacles that threatened our marriage, but God resolved them all. I was blessed with a wonderful job. We exchanged vows on July 15, 1995, which happened to be the hottest day of that year. Our wedding colors were black and white. My baby girl and stepson served as the flower girl and ring bearer, while my oldest daughter was a junior bridesmaid, and my son was a junior groomsman. Some of my cousins, my husband's friends, and my pastor attended the wedding. Interestingly, our next-door neighbor served as my maid of honor. It was a beautiful wedding, and I felt like Cinderella. My dress was white with a sequined train, and it flared out like a Cinderella gown. We were filled with joy as we embarked on our new life together. We purchased a new home and were incredibly happy. About four years later, the kids and I went back to visit our old home. It was the second time I saw their father since he had been released from prison. I took the children to see him at his trailer. While they went inside for a few minutes, my cousin and I waited in the van. Finally, the kids came out, and I caught a glimpse of him. As we drove away, I broke down and started crying, and so did my children. There was a gospel song playing that said, "Lord, thank you for saving me from me." When I returned home, I asked my pastor why I felt that way upon seeing him, and he explained that God had given me a compassionate heart. The forgiveness I now had for him made me cry, not only for myself but also for his soul to be saved. That trip was a healing journey for all of us. Each time I visited, people didn't recognize me. Some had even assumed I was dead.

We went to a restaurant one day, and I happened to see a girl there whom I had gone to school with. I greeted her and asked how she was doing, and she responded. Then I mentioned that I was Vanessa Ford, and she exclaimed, "Oh my God! Look at you! I thought Vanessa had died years ago." I was taken aback by her response. Another time, I visited the hospital and one of the supervisors there looked me in the face and said, "I do not remember you." I had truly transformed into a whole new person. On occasion, we would visit the kids' aunts, and their father would be present.

As my children grew older, they desired a relationship with their father. I never turned them against him. I believed that was a decision they should make for themselves. One year, my oldest daughter asked if she could bring him to our house for Thanksgiving. I agreed, knowing she wanted to mend things with him. She now has our beautiful granddaughter. So that Thanksgiving, she and my son brought their dad to Pennsylvania. At my house, I cooked the entire dinner, and my husband was fine with it. As I prepared the meal, I prayed.

On Thanksgiving day, we took the food over to their father's place. I remember feeling a little nervous as I approached the door, but I took a deep breath and asked God for help. My husband and I went inside, exchanged greetings, and engaged in conversation. When it was time to eat, we all sat at the table, and I blessed the food. It turned out to be a pleasant occasion. We reminisced about the past, talked about our granddaughter, and enjoyed each other's company. Then the evening came to an end, and we praised God. The kids wanted their father to attend church, but he refused. When my son graduated, he wanted to go back home and try to reconcile with his dad. I accompanied him on that trip.

During our visit, we were at the aunt's house when their father and his friend came over. I remember sharing my testimony with him that day. I asked if he had ever heard of T. D. Jakes, and he said no. I told him about the influential preacher and how, if he allowed God to save him, he could lead others to Christ. I emphasized that God can take someone with a tarnished reputation and accomplish great things through them. I continued to speak to him about the goodness of God. His friend remarked, "Man, who is this woman?" He replied, "Man, she's the mother of my children. Back in the day, she and I were true troopers." Then he said,

"Today I don't know who she is. She's not the same woman I knew." I replied, "It's because of Jesus living in me."

Candis once told me, "Mama, I never got to know the Vanessa Ford that everyone else knew. I wish I had, but that Vanessa Ford is dead, and God has created a whole new person. Vanessa Taylor now lives." Those words brought tears to my eyes because as I reflect on my life, I realize that I am a new creature. Although I still have areas that God is working on in my life, I understand that I am not perfect and that it is a daily journey. However, for the most part, God has brought about a 360-degree turnaround in my life. Sometimes, this transformation can feel a little daunting. Pumpkin and Pong and I discuss it at times. When we view our lives from a worldly perspective, it seems as though we were transplanted to Pennsylvania and became entirely new individuals with a fresh identity. However, there are moments when we return to our hometown, and it feels like our spirits attempt to reconnect with who we used to be. A friend once remarked that our bodies may have left Fayetteville, but our spirits still have a connection there. I am grateful to God for the person I am today. I have discovered my true identity.

CHAPTER 13

Realizing My Purpose

And we know that all things work together for good to them that love God, to them who are the called according to his purpose. For whom he did foreknow, he also did predestinate to be conformed to the image of his Son, that he might be the firstborn among many brethren.
—Romans 8:28–29

All that I endured in life was not in vain; I now understand that God is using my life as a testimony to others, drawing lost souls to Him. There are many women who have gone through similar experiences as mine, but unfortunately, some of them are no longer alive to share their stories. I believe that I was destined to fulfill my current purpose, which is living for Christ and spreading the gospel through my testimony.

In this chapter, I will discuss the following:

- The woman I have become after undergoing transformation
- My children and the impact of my journey on their lives

- The support and love I receive from my husband
- The encounters I've had with individuals whose lives have been changed by hearing my testimony
- The ongoing work that God is doing in and through me

As I wrote about my previous out-of-body experience, I realized it was the beginning of God revealing His purpose for my life. The challenges and trials I had faced since childhood were all part of His plan. The moment I knew with certainty that He had called me to share my survivor testimony was when a lady I knew started a girls' group. She was seeking individuals to share personal stories that could potentially impact the girls' futures. I had never spoken about being a survivor before. She said, "Vanessa, you have something to share, and I believe it will greatly benefit these girls." I felt scared and nervous. I prayed and sought God's guidance, and He assured me that it was indeed His will. Around the same time, I joined another church with a powerful pastor who frequently told me, "Sis Vanessa, God is going to use you in extraordinary ways. Your story will reach people all over the world." He confirmed that speaking was my calling, and I embraced it.

One thing I can say about my pastor, who has since passed away and is with the Lord, is that he spoke many things into my life, and today I see them coming to pass. However, I want to share about a specific Sunday evening when I was scheduled to speak. That Sunday morning, I woke up feeling sick. My throat was hurting, and I was beginning to lose my voice. I thought to myself, "Oh my God, what is happening?" Despite feeling unwell, we got dressed and went to church. As my condition worsened, I couldn't even sing in the choir that day. I approached the pastor in the prayer line and shared what was happening. He laid hands on me, prayed, and said, "Have faith, God is going to use you tonight, and He will receive the glory."

So I went home, but my condition continued to deteriorate. My family asked me what I was going to do. I told them that I was going to lay down and take a nap, and see what God would say when I woke up. After fixing dinner and feeding my family, I lay down. A few hours later, I woke up, and it had gotten worse. I could barely whisper. My daughters asked, "Mom, what are you going to do?" I replied, "I'm going to believe God and go." So my daughters and I got dressed and headed to the event.

When I arrived, I met with the lady and gentleman who were in charge of the program. Honestly, I could barely utter a whisper. We joined hands, and they began to pray, asking God to open my windpipes so that I could speak. The program began, and my daughter introduced me, explaining that I could barely talk but had faith that I would be able to share my story. I got up, and I'm telling you, God can perform miracles. Though I started off whispering due to my limited ability to speak, as I began to tell my story, God opened my windpipes and gave me just enough breath to share my testimony. When I finished, my throat closed back up. It was truly amazing! The girls in attendance witnessed the glory of God that day, and many of them began to open up and share their own experiences and the hurts they had endured. We had a time of prayer, and I believe that not only was my life touched, but theirs as well. My daughters and I left, praising God for the powerful move of His Spirit.

The next day, I went to the doctor and was diagnosed with laryngitis. It was in that moment that I knew I was called to share my story. I contacted the women's center, and they introduced me to a detective at the courthouse who specialized in domestic violence cases. I remember sitting at a table with an advocate from the women's center and the two detectives, who were the head investigators for domestic violence cases. They were eager to hear my story.

I began to share my story, and after I finished, one of the detectives looked at me and said, "God is going to use your story." I turned to him in surprise and said, "Excuse me," to which he responded, "God is going to use your story." I was in awe, realizing that hearing those words from a detective truly affirmed that God had a purpose for me. He advised me to take some classes at the women's center so that I could volunteer my services there. I met a young lady who has been a strong support in everything I do, always encouraging me to keep going. She worked at the shelter at that time and is now a legal advocate. She would arrange for me to come and share my story at the shelters. It was a wonderful experience, and I started organizing Christmas dinners for the women after sharing, as well as fundraising to buy gifts for them and their children. Even during Valentine's Day, I would go and have lunch with them, bringing candy to share. I saw it as an opportunity to show them love and care, knowing that they were hurting.

Many doors opened up for me to share my story, and many lives were touched, both men and women. I appeared on a few television shows and spoke at women's conferences in prisons, among other engagements. Then one day the Lord spoke to me and said I needed a title when I went out to speak. I used to listen to Daryl Coley, an anointed singer, and he has a song called "Mask." This song resonated with me, and I had my children listen to it. They said, "Mom, that is it—'Mask.'" But as I prayed about it, the Lord added to it and said, "From Behind the Mask," to convey the message to women that they need to remove the mask of their past and open up to God's healing. Many of us walk around every day, appearing as if we have it all together, but when night falls and no one is around, we find ourselves lying in a pool of tears, hurting from the wounds of our past. For me, forgiveness was the key. If I had not surrendered my life to God and truly forgiven my abuser, I would not be free to tell my story today. I love the quote that says, "To set a prisoner free is forgiveness, and the prisoner it releases is you." I had held myself captive to the chains of my past. Unforgiveness has that power. Since that first speaking engagement, God has opened so many doors for me to share my story. I have spoken at numerous conferences, appeared on a few gospel television networks, visited prisons, and had many one-on-one conversations.

The conference I spoke at that had a profound impact on many people was called "Shake the Foundation." It took place at a church, and the female minister invited me to come and share my story. My cousin, who is also in ministry, called me and said, "God said tonight is going to be different; many people will be set free." I was incredibly nervous, but my husband reassured me, saying, "You will be fine." I had requested that a friend from church sing Pastor Shirley Caesar's song, "You're Next in Line for a Miracle." Additionally, I had a dream where I saw myself speaking at a specific venue, and I envisioned how everything would be set up. In the dream, I witnessed people running and praising God, exclaiming, "I'm free!" They urged me not to stop telling my story because it would help others. When I arrived at the church that night, it was set up exactly as I had seen it in the dream. My friend sang, and then I took the stage to share. It always feels like God allows me to deliver my message in a different way each time. On this particular night, God used me in such a mighty way that it left me in awe. At the end of my sharing, there was an altar call, and men, women, young, and old came forward for prayer. Some were crying, while others praised God, declaring their freedom. It was just as my cousin had foretold. I know that people left that place transformed.

Another instance was a divine setup orchestrated by God. A lady from work and I attended a meeting where she met the president of an organization that assists children who come from troubled homes. She introduced me to this lady, and we struck up a conversation. Almost instantly, we exchanged numbers, and within a few weeks, I was invited to speak at their facility. The day came for me to go and share my story, and it was located approximately an hour away from where I lived. I had never been to that town before. That morning, I kissed my husband goodbye and began my drive. As I was driving, I heard the Lord tell me to put on Juanita Bynum's worship CD. It was one of her worship albums. I played the CD and found myself worshiping along as I drove. Around ten minutes later, I found myself right in front of a car dealership, and suddenly, my car shut down. Everything just stopped. I managed to coast to the side of the road, and my car completely shut off.

As it stopped, a man who worked there pulled up and asked what was wrong. I told him I didn't know, but everything had just shut down, and I had to be at a speaking engagement shortly. He reassured me not to worry, as they would help me. I witnessed something incredible. He pushed my car into the lot and called their mechanic. They arrived and took my car. They directed me to the courtesy room and told me to have a seat while they arranged a ride for me. Then another man approached and asked where I needed to go. I told him, and he said, "No problem, I know where it is. I'll take you right there." Meanwhile, the first gentleman came back and assured me not to worry because they were fixing my car. I called my husband and said, "This is crazy, and we don't have a dime." I also called the lady I was supposed to speak for, updating her on the situation. I realized it was the devil trying to stop me every time I had to speak. She responded, "No problem, we will be waiting." I got into a nice vehicle with the older gentleman, and we began the ride. I couldn't help but smile, thinking, "This is amazing." We arrived at the place, and he handed me a card, saying, "Just call when you're done, and I'll come back to pick you up." Look at God! I entered the venue and was warmly greeted by everyone. I started my engagement, and it went well with many positive responses.

What I didn't know was that I was there for the people God had sent me to, including the lady I had met earlier. This day was meant for her to be set free. She approached me after I made some calls to check on my car. They informed me that the repair cost would be over $300. I exclaimed, "Oh my God, I don't have that kind of money with me." The lady responded, "Well, we usually don't do this, but we'll issue a check for you today. I hope it can help you." I opened the envelope, and there it was—a check for $350. I marveled at God's provision. I wasn't expecting that at all. Then she invited me into her office and asked me to have a seat. As I sat in that big, beautiful office with the company president, I was amazed at everything that had transpired. She began to speak and said, "You really helped me today." Tears started rolling down her face. She shared about a past relationship that still haunted her, despite having since gotten married and had a baby. The position she held was significant, yet she was still bound by the baggage from her past. I told her that today she had removed her mask, and God had initiated a healing process. It was a truly beautiful moment.

My ride arrived, and I cashed the check to pay for my car. I drove back home, giving praise to God for His goodness. There have been many other instances where I've witnessed God working in similar ways. Before I go to speak, I always say, "Jesus, me and You have a date." The devil has tried to stop me, but I keep going. Not only did I start my ministry, but I also established the Ford Foundation. It offers the Vanessa Ford Scholarship in my maiden name to a child who has been affected by domestic violence. I awarded my first scholarship in June 2012. I love everything I do for domestic violence. My family is incredibly supportive. My husband stands behind me and encourages me to continue the work. I am proud of my children. They are also very supportive, and there have been times when I've had them speak as well. I believe it's healing for them too. It makes me feel good because despite all they've been through, they have turned out to be exceptional men and women.

My son, Pong, pursued a career in culinary arts. Even when he was in school, students and teachers would say that he always talked about becoming a chef. He has a passion for cooking, and today he is a talented sous chef. My oldest daughter, Pumpkin, has blessed me with two beautiful grandchildren—a boy named Ace and a girl named Aniya. She is a hardworking and devoted mother, and I can see her writing a book one day. Candis is currently working as a CNA nurse and is studying to pursue a career in the medical field. They are the greatest children anyone could ask for, and I feel truly blessed to have such a wonderful family. Sometimes I laugh because I'm always coming up with new ideas, whether it's for a fundraiser or to spread awareness about domestic violence. I know they may think, "Here she goes again," but nevertheless, they are always there to support me because they know this is my purpose and destiny—it's in my heart. Pumpkin tells people that her mom is a superhero. I have encountered wonderful people in my life who have encouraged me to pursue things I never thought I could do. I am heavily involved in the labor movement and politics. I am also actively engaged in my church, participating in the choir and women's ministry.

When it was laid on my heart to write my life story, a song came to mind. I know Gladys Knight has sung the song, but I believe James Cleveland has also. The song is titled "The Best Thing That Ever Happened to Me." Just tell them that JESUS is the best thing that ever happened to me. It's a true statement—when He came into my life, I began to truly live. As for their father, he is still living in the South. Whenever we go to visit, the kids always go to see him, and I often see him as well. We greet each other with a hello and talk about the grandchildren briefly. I will say, it's sad to see him.

A year ago, during a family reunion visit, there was a particular morning when I said to my husband that I just needed some time to ride. This is what I do when I go home—I simply drive around and look at the places where I used to stay and reminisce. That morning, I turned on the gospel station, and they were playing "If It Had Not Been for the Lord on My Side." I began to cry, thanking God. Then the Lord started directing me as I was driving. I was planning to get my favorite biscuit from Biscuit Kitchen, but He said, "No, go this way." As I followed His guidance, I looked to my left and saw the kids' father. He didn't see me, but I saw him. My heart broke when I saw how he had aged and lost so much weight. He looked as if life was ready to leave him any day. The song was still playing, and I continued to cry, saying, "God, thank You, but God, save him."

I arrived at Biscuit Kitchen, but I couldn't place an order because I was crying so hard. I called my daughter Pumpkin and told her that I had just seen her dad, and, oh my God, he looked so bad. She began to talk to me, trying to calm me down. After I got off the phone, the lady behind the counter asked if I was okay, and I said to her, "If you only knew." I was crying out in thanks, but at the same time, asking God to save someone's soul who, at one time, almost took my life. I left and went back to the hotel where my husband and family were, and as I was driving back, the Lord then told me to turn right at the stoplights. When I did, I looked and saw a big tent with a lot of people standing around, and a sign saying, "Lord is Lord" and so forth. They were feeding the people and trying to spread the Word for them to be saved. I looked, and there was my children's father. I drove halfway down the street and just sat where I couldn't be seen. I watched and watched, and I said, "Oh my God," and I began to cry again. All I could think was, "If it had not been for the Lord on my side, tell me, where would I be?" I still pray for him today.

See, when you have truly forgiven someone, you also find yourself praying for them. I continue to share my story and show the picture to prove that I am a survivor and that God is GOOD!

Vanessa Ford-Taylor is a triumphant survivor of domestic violence. She is an inspirational/ motivational speaker who has dedicated her life to helping victims of domestic violence. Her story has helped a multitude of victims become victorious in conquering overwhelming obstacles.

Vanessa began sharing her testimony in the year 2000 at various community groups, women's conferences, male prisons, as well as appearing on Christian television shows and radio stations. She has received many awards in the community for her work.

Through her many speaking engagements, Vanessa was inspired to found her ministry, From Behind the Mask, in 2001. With this ministry, she shares her story, courage, strength, and blessings in the hope of providing a step towards healing for those in need. She reaches out to men and women of all ages. In 2011, she started the Ford Foundation, a nonprofit organization in her maiden name, which provides help for families affected by domestic violence and recovering addicts.

The Ford Foundation successfully completed their first Candy Cane Village in December 2023. A total of twenty-five families with thirty-one children in the surrounding area of Beaver County, provided each child gifts they had requested on their application.

In September 2016, she hosted her first heroin and opiates awareness event called "Can You Reach My Friend?" In 2019, she began a ministry called Bag Lady that helps women or men recognize the years of baggage they have carried and empowers them to become free, so they can live a life healed from past hurts.

Vanessa is the mother of Shanicka DeWarron (Pong) and Candis Ford. She has two grandchildren, Aniya and Ace, and great-grandsons Sante and Arison. She has been married to her love, Robert Taylor, for twenty-eight years. She is a member and ministry in training to become an Evangelist at Deliverance COGIC under Bishop Marvin Moreland.

In November 2022, she won a seat on the city council of the town she currently lives in, Beaver Falls, where she will hold a four-year term.

Today she shares how she is able to forgive her abuser because it is the only way she can cope with her past and live in the present. Her motto is, "To forgive is to set free that which was held prisoner, and that which was set free is you." Vanessa credits her recovery from her injuries and addiction to the grace of God, who is her strength, and without Him, none of her work would be possible. She is truly an overcomer.

www.ingramcontent.com/pod-product-compliance
Lightning Source LLC
Chambersburg PA
CBHW022021150726
47990CB00002B/749